WHY Can't I Get My Kids to BEHAVE?

Joey and Carla Link

WestBow
PRESS
A DIVISION OF THOMAS NELSON

ISBN: 978-1-4497-7283-3(sc)
ISBN: 978-1-4497-7284-0(hc)
ISBN: 978-1-4497-7282-6(e)

Library of Congress Control Number: 2012922246

WestBow Press books may be ordered through booksellers or by contacting:

WestBow Press
A Division of Thomas Nelson
1663 Liberty Drive
Bloomington, IN 47403
www.westbowpress.com
1-(866) 928-1240

Printed in the United States of America

WestBow Press rev. date:11/27/2012

CONTENTS

PRAISE FOR "WHY CAN'T I GET MY KIDS TO BEHAVE?" IX

WHY CAN'T I GET MY KIDS TO BEHAVE? 1

WHAT OBEDIENCE IS 13

THE PARENTING TOOLBOX 31

WHAT OBEDIENCE IS NOT 56

FIRST THINGS FIRST 67

KEEP PLUGGING AWAY 81

DO COMPLIANT KIDS EXIST? 93

DON'T USE THIS TOOLBOX! 108

IT'S NOT TOO LATE 125

NOTES 137

ADDITIONAL RESOURCES BY JOEY AND CARLA LINK 143

PARENTING RESOURCES   RECOMMENDED BY JOEY AND CARLA

LINK 145

ABOUT THE AUTHORS 147

To our children, Michael, Briana, and Amy—
Your lives are a blessing to us and have far exceeded
our highest expectations as parents. You are the living
testimonies of our faith in biblical principles and how they
apply to every area of our lives.

To Rachael, Dan, and Nathan—
Thank you for loving our kids and for joining our
family.

And to Hudson Adams Link—
You are the first of the next generation of our family.
Your parents named you for Samuel Adams, your
great-great-great grandfather, who went into China with
Hudson Taylor, leaving you with a spiritual legacy that
will enrich your life.

The apostle John said it best when he wrote in 3 John 1:4,

*"I have no greater joy than to hear that my children are
walking in the truth."*

PRAISE FOR "WHY CAN'T I GET MY KIDS TO BEHAVE?"

Have you ever wanted an instruction manual for parenting? Look no further. This is the book you've been waiting for. With refreshing honesty and practical instruction, Joey and Carla Link have put together a great resource for parents. If you have kids, you need this book.

—Jill Savage, founder and CEO of Hearts at Home,
author of *No More Perfect Moms*

The biblical and practical teaching Joey and Carla Link share is something every parent should read. It has given us clear expectations—what we as parents can require of our kids and what our kids know is expected of them. We are confident this book will be a good beginning for parents, no matter the ages of their children.

—US Representative Bill (and Natalie) Huizenga, Michigan

Practical, inspiring, encouraging, and vision-forming, this book is a powerful tool for parents. Joey and Carla Link do a beautiful job of imparting both the why and how of biblical parenting. The principles they share in this book have made an incredible impact in our home.

—Eric and Leslie Ludy, best-selling authors
of *When God Writes Your Love Story*

Being a pediatrician for over thirty years, I can't think of a parent who hasn't wanted his or her children to behave. I have known Joey and Carla for many years and have personally observed them raise their children. By getting into the heart of the child and the dynamics of the family, they have given us practical tools to raise obedient children. I can enthusiastically recommend this book to families in my medical practice.

—Jim Pearson, MD

ACKNOWLEDGMENTS

First and most of all, we thank our Lord and Savior, Jesus Christ, for determining we are worthy of the privilege of serving Him by ministering to families. The words "*Thank you*" are not adequate to show our gratitude to Him as well as to those who have been mentors in our lives in the realms of spiritual growth and parenting.

Greg Barnett, you saw promise in me (Joey) when few others did. You have been a consistent example pointing me to follow Jesus. You taught me what faithfulness, loyalty, and integrity look like. You officiated our wedding and told us then that you believed we would serve the Lord better together than apart. God obviously agreed, as we are still serving Him together as one in ministry thirty-four years later.

My (Joey's) dad, Charlie Link, taught me to be there for my kids, to always find a way to root them on in whatever they chose to do, and to find a way to help them succeed. He left us just shy of his ninetieth birthday, and we all miss his encouraging smile to this day.

My (Carla's) mom, Mary C. Siemens, left me a legacy of spiritual mentoring. She led by example more than words. My mother showed me how to persevere through difficult times with grace and dignity, keeping my faith intact. Mom and Granddaddy left us weeks apart, and are both joyfully living with our Lord now. We would be remiss to not mention them with grateful hearts.

We want to thank Gary and Anne Marie Ezzo for believing in us over twenty years ago. We are grateful you have been there for us on our parenting journey, mentoring us in biblical parenting and always showing us the light at the end of the tunnel. Your wisdom and experience prepared us to parent our own children, which gave us the confidence and ability to assist others by giving them hope and encouragement in the often overwhelming task of parenting.

We thank our daughter Amy Carpenter for her photography work on the cover design and her husband Nathan, our technical wizard. We give special thanks to David and Renee Sproles and their children for being willing to model for the picture on the front cover. Don't be fooled by the picture— they really are great kids!

We are grateful to those who wrote chapter testimonies and the endorsements for us. We trust your example will bless many.

Finally, to all the parents across the globe who have trusted us to assist them with the raising of their children through our teaching, counseling, and the *Mom's Notes* presentations, thank you for allowing us the privilege of serving you.

INTRODUCTION

Why should you read *Why Can't I Get My Kids to Behave?*
Parents often ask us:

- How they can get their child to stay in a chair for a
  time-out

- If they should even bother giving their children chores
  because they can't get them to do them

- If they can get through a day without wanting to pull
  their hair out!

We will answer all of these.

Why Can't I Get My Kids to Behave? uses biblical principles
to give practical suggestions for dealing with the root causes
for your children's poor behavior. The goal of this book is
to look at what an obedient child is and share how to get
your children to obey. If your children obey you, they will
behave.

Parenting is an awesome blessing, but it is also a huge
responsibility. Just as time slips through our fingers on a
daily basis, so does the opportunity you have to teach, train,
and raise your children. It is our hope and prayer that by
the time you finish reading this book you will be able to say
with confidence that you know how to raise a child who
will behave.

When I (Joey) first started in full-time pastoral ministry
to families, I spent a lot of time looking for a proactive
parenting curriculum. I was referred to Growing Families

Int'l, and after attending a conference they sponsored, Carla and I started using their parenting curriculum in our home and church. The teaching in this material is based on biblical principles, and that greatly appealed to us both, for the Bible is the one book that will never change.

Many of the foundational principles shared in *Why Can't I Get My Kids to Behave?* are based on teaching in the *Growing Kids God's Way* parenting curriculum and are used with the authors' permission and blessing.

We are often asked if our children are aware of the stories we share about their childhood and adolescence when we teach and write. They know we share stories about them, and we have their blessing to do so.

At the end of each chapter you will find a testimony from a family who has used the material we are sharing with their children for many years. We personally know the children represented by these families and have watched most of them grow from toddlers to the teenagers and college students they are today. They are a blessing to know.

To keep things simple, we have used the pronoun "he" to represent children in the text. It is by no means gender specific. We don't want you to get the impression that we think only boys misbehave.

Study questions for each chapter of this book can be downloaded at www.parentingmadepractical.com. Posts on parenting topics by Joey and Carla Link can be found here also.

CHAPTER 1

WHY CAN'T I GET MY KIDS TO BEHAVE?

"**M**om!" six-year-old Scott yelled. "I don't want to put my toys away. I'm not done playing with them yet. I'm not gonna put them away!"

"Oh, yes, you are," his mom told him as she walked toward him, picking up toys as she went along. She handed Scott a pile of toy trucks. "Put these in that bin now!"

Scott threw the toys in the bin and ran to the kitchen. "I'm hungry and want my sandwich."

"Get back here and pick up the rest of your toys, or you won't get lunch," Mom said as she continued to pick up toys.

"I don't need you," Scott hollered at her. "I can make my sandwich myself!"

His mom hurried to the kitchen as she heard a chair scraping across the floor. She wasn't surprised to find her son sitting on the counter pulling the peanut butter out of the cupboard when she got there. She pulled Scott off the counter and made him a sandwich.

While Scott was munching away, not expecting a response she asked, "Why can't you behave?"

Mom went back to the family room to pick up the rest of Scott's toys, wishing he still took naps so she could have some peace and quiet in her day.

***

Later that day, the neighbor who lived across the street went into her thirteen-year-old daughter's bedroom to check and see if she was doing her homework. Kate was laying on her bed texting friends on her phone. Her mom told her to get her schoolwork done. Kate responded by telling her she would get to it later.

"Later," replied her mother, "you never get around to it later."

"I said I would get to it later!" Kate retorted. "Now leave me alone."

"Leave you alone?" cried her mom. "Fine, I will leave you alone. I'm going to check, and if you don't have your homework done before school tomorrow, I am taking away your phone."

"Fine, take it away," Kate yelled. "You'll just give it back to me because you want to call me whenever the mood strikes you."

"Don't you smart-mouth me young lady," her mom said through clenched teeth. "I will take away whatever I want and keep it as long as I want."

Kate picked up her backpack and dumped the books inside it on her bed. She plopped down and opened one of the textbooks. She told her mom to get out of her room and she would get her homework done by dinner. Her mother sighed as she left the room.

***

Do these scenarios sound familiar? Expectant parents are so excited when their little bundle of joy finally arrives. All too soon, that adorable baby turns into a toddler who one day stomps his foot and yells "No!" when he isn't getting his own way. Frustrated parents, not knowing what else to do, give in to the child's demands.

If you fast-forward through the elementary and middle school years, you will find scenarios similar to Scott and Kate's are common in your home. Next come the teen years, where you rarely see your child once he gets his driver's license. Are you wondering if it is possible to get through these years without living through teenage rebellion?

Will a child who does not know how to behave make it in college? Failure to teach your children how to obey will affect every stage of their life, and they will become totally independent before they are emotionally, intellectually, and socially ready for it.

Last Christmas, Joey and I were standing in a long line in a department store waiting to check out. The girl at the cash register was talking loudly to a friend who had stopped to greet her. Everyone in line could hear their conversation.

Her friend asked the salesgirl, "Are you staying home for Christmas?"

"Are you kidding?" said the salesgirl. "That is the last place I want to be. Talk about boring! I'm going skiing in Colorado with my boyfriend."

"I am not staying home either," said her friend. "I'm going to Mexico to celebrate beach life with friends."

Joey and I walked away, feeling a deep sadness for the parents of these girls. We could imagine the parents planning a time of fun and celebration for the holiday season, desperately hoping their kids will want to spend the time with them.

How did it get to this in our society today? Parents give their kids everything they want and more and pay their way through expensive colleges to find out their kids don't want to be with them. Sounds depressing, doesn't it? You surely weren't expecting this when you decided to have kids.

We believe you don't have to settle for this with your kids. You can have more. All three of our children and their spouses tell us they enjoy coming to our home to visit us. It is a fun time of talking, playing games, relaxing, and being together. We don't see each other often, as our kids live in three different states across the country, so everyone looks forward to the times we are able to get together. We all support and encourage one another however we can.

Do you want your children to grow into adults who are characterized by spiritual, emotional, and material success?

Imagine it is the Olympic Games. Your child is a long-distance runner. You have spent years doing little else but prepare him for this race. You taught him how to run correctly so his muscles work in perfect harmony. You have emphasized the importance of eating a healthy diet so his body will be at its best. Your child no longer lets other things, as good as they may be, take his focus off his goal. The race is starting, and he is in position with the other runners, waiting for the starting gun to go off.

What is the starting gun for the race this child will run one day? Believe it or not, it all goes back to the way you parent him. The way you parent your children is the training they get for the all-important race of life.

The starting gun for any Olympic race is *obedience*. All athletes who participate in an Olympic event have to obey their coaches or they would never make it to the games. The stronger the foundation you lay in your children's hearts of their need to obey people in authority, the greater their levels of endurance and perseverance will be to finish the race ahead of the pack.

What is Obedience?

If you were to ask ten people what obedience is, they would all most likely come to the same conclusion, doing what you are told to do. However, you would likely hear ten different ways to accomplish this.

Based on the definition "doing what you are told to do," did either Scott or Kate obey? Do you think their moms think Scott and Kate obeyed? They did make a halfhearted effort to comply, but we are guessing their parents did not see this as true obedience. Why? Obedience is more than just doing what you are told to do. True obedience also includes *how* you do it.

Authority is Not a Bad Word

In our culture today, if you hear the word "authority," it is often used in a negative way. Many connotations of the word "authority" are mentioned in the dictionary. The connotations all have one thing in common. Basically, "authority" means *"the power to act."*[1]

You can obtain this right through a title that designates a role, such as an employer, teacher, or parent. You can also earn the right to have the power to act by gaining the respect of those under you.

Why can't parents get their children to behave? Based on this definition, it is logical to assume parents have abdicated their "power to act" on behalf of their kids. In other words, kids are the authority in their homes, not the parents. Whoever has the ultimate control in your home is the authority and has claimed the right to rule the roost.

When we visited my (Carla's) grandparents, one of our kids' favorite things to do was go see the chicken coop that was on the property where they lived. The rooster unquestionably ruled the roost. No announcement or proclamation had to be made. No sign hung over the coop letting everyone know this. All one had to do was watch the hens to figure out who was in control. They obeyed the rooster's every command.

Are you the rooster in your home? Do each of your children think they are the rooster? How can you get your kids to behave? If you are the rooster, your kids will become the chickens and they will do what you tell them to do.

Obedience Defined

To "obey" is *"to conform to or comply with an order; to be controlled by; to follow the guidance of another."*[2] How many children like for someone else to control them? What child wants to follow the guidance of another person, especially his parents? Children don't want to comply with an order, for doing so means relinquishing control. Very few people, no matter what their age, like giving up control.

Even though few of us want someone else to control us, somewhere along the way we got the idea that our children will let us run their lives and they will do what we say without argument. This gene is not in anyone's genetic pool.

God spoke specifically through the apostle Paul in Ephesians 6:1. *"Children obey your parents in the Lord for this is right."* God expects children to obey. He doesn't hope they will, want them to or keep His fingers crossed. He expects them to, no ifs or buts about it. Not only does He expect children to obey their parents, He goes on to say, just in case anyone thinks this is unfair, that this is right.

Children will not understand how to obey God unless they first learn to obey their parents. How do your children learn to obey? This verse says God gave every child a parent to teach him what authority looks like and how to obey those who have authority in his life.

Children must learn to obey before they will submit. Children obey because they have to (their fear of consequences). They submit because they want to (because it is the right thing to do). This hardly applies to children only.

When any of us see a police car sitting on the side of the road, if we are driving over the speed limit we immediately hit the brakes to slow down so we will not get a ticket. We don't want to get a ticket because we don't want to pay the fine or have it put on our driving record (the fear of consequences).

From Adam and Eve to us, God has given everyone the freedom to choose to be controlled by someone in authority, the freedom to *choose* to obey. We have the freedom to choose to obey?

I (Joey) was frustrated with our son Michael. Being a teenager and thinking he knew it all, Michael was arguing with me. I told him, "You are choosing to disobey!" By the look he gave me when I said this, I knew I was on to something.

Telling a child, "You didn't obey" is one thing. With this statement, whose court is the ball in? The parents are holding the ball. Telling a child, "You chose to disobey" tosses the ball back into his court. Our children's responses when we started saying, "Did you choose to obey?" told us that adding the word "choose" to their obedience or lack of was powerful.

Choosing to Obey

It doesn't matter what age kids are, they get to choose to obey or not. Your child is two years old. He is banging his cup on the high chair, demanding you give him more milk to drink. You have been working with him to say "please."

He refuses to cooperate, so you decide he won't have any more milk because he won't say "please." He immediately says "please," and you give him the milk (which you should do at this age). Did he choose to obey? Not at first, but when given the option of not getting any milk, he changed his mind.

There is a terrific story in the Bible of a boy named Samuel. When he was around the age of seven years old,[3] his mother took him to live with a wise, godly man named Eli so he could learn how to grow up and serve God. One night, Samuel thought he heard Eli calling him. He got up, ran to where Eli was sleeping, and said, "Here I am. You called me!"

Eli must have thought the boy was having a dream because he didn't call him, so he sent Samuel back to bed. Not long after, Samuel heard his name called again. For the second time, he jumped up, ran, and woke up Eli.

"Here I am. You called me!"

Once again, Eli sent him back to his bed, wondering what Samuel thought he was hearing. Samuel went back to bed, probably wondering himself what was going on.

Samuel had barely gotten to sleep when he heard his name called a third time. He jumped up, ran, and woke up Eli once again.

"Here I am. You called me!"

Because no one else was in the area, Eli realized God was calling the boy. He told Samuel how to respond if he heard his name called again.

Sure enough, Samuel heard his name called for the fourth time. He said the words Eli had given him, *"Speak, for your servant hears"* (1 Samuel 3:10).

8

God was calling Samuel, for He was teaching him to respond immediately when God called his name. Why did God keep calling Samuel when the boy came every time he heard his name called? God had big plans for Samuel, and He needed to be sure Samuel would listen to Him without question, not only the first time, but every time He called him.

Now, do you think Samuel was an extraordinary boy who thought he should run to Eli whenever he called him to see what he wanted? We don't think so. We are sure his mother Hannah taught him how to respond when he heard his name called before she took him to the temple to live.

The story of Samuel is a great one to read to your kids, especially when you are teaching them what obeying looks like. You can find this story in 1 Samuel 3:1–11.

Have you ever thought about calling your child's name and waiting for a response? We first heard this concept at a parenting conference we attended when our kids were young. We decided to try it when we got home, but I (Joey) was not sure I thought it would make a difference.

Not only did it make a difference, when our children decided not to respond in a positive way when they heard their names called, they were much easier to deal with because they were not yet too far out of control. The kids quickly came back under control after we stepped in to deal with it. This alone made our lives much easier and our home more peaceful.

Another reason parents should teach their children to respond to the call of their name immediately was brought home to our community in a profound way. A four-year-old boy was outside with his dad, who was doing yard work. The boy often wandered away as his dad was focused on the work he was doing. Dad looked up and saw his son running after a ball that was rolling toward the street.

Dad called his son's name, but he didn't stop. Dad ran to get him and pulled him off the street, telling him to stay put in the yard. A short time later, the boy ran out into the street again when his dad wasn't looking. His dad looked up when he heard a car's engine and called his son's name. Once again, his son ignored him and was run over by the neighbor as he was backing out of the driveway. Sadly, he was killed.

Teaching your child to come to you at the call of his name could very well save his life.

Are We Expecting Too Much?

Getting your child to come at the call of his name is the greatest foundation you can put in place when you train your child to obey. It is also one of the greatest challenges you will face in parenting, for you are teaching your children the importance of agreeing to do what they don't want to do.

Bethany's parents have been working on training her and her siblings to obey and submit to God's principles for living all of their lives. Bethany had been sick for a month when a medical team found she was suffering from a potentially debilitating disease.

After getting the diagnosis, twelve-year-old Bethany spent a month in the hospital going through many difficult and painful tests. The medical team working with her was surprised and in awe not only of her overall attitude, but mostly by her level of compliance to all she was asked to submit to.

How could Bethany's parents know, when they started training her so long ago she would desperately need this training when she was so young? Because of the training she received from her parents, as a preteen, she was ready to respond when God called her name.

Bethany and her family believed when God said in Romans 8:28, *"We know that in all things God works for the good of those who love him, who have been called according to his purpose,"* He meant having this disease was for this family's good.

What is good about it? How Bethany and her family live with this disease is a light that shines for God's eternal glory because the darker your path, the more people pay attention to you.

We know this is hard for people to understand on this side of eternity. When we are all in heaven one day, it will become crystal clear why God chose paths of pain and suffering for some Christians when we see all those who are celebrating the glory of eternal life because they came to know Christ as their Savior at the expense of someone's pain. Bethany was ready to respond to God's call. Will your child be ready to obey when, for whatever reason, God calls his name?

When my (Joey's) dad was eighty-nine years old, I flew to where he lived in Southern California to take him to a Los Angeles Lakers basketball game for his Christmas present that year. My dad was a lifelong fan, and I had wanted to take him to a game for a long time. We were on the edge of our seats as the game went into double overtime.

With just three seconds on the clock, the Lakers coach called a time-out to go over one final play. When the coach called the play, he knew exactly where each of the five players who were on the court needed to be. He told the players what to do and how to do it. Each player had a choice. He could do what the coach had just instructed him to do, or choose to do his own thing.

Because they had been trained to do what the coach told them to do, the players followed the play perfectly and won the game at the sound of the buzzer. My dad and I were overjoyed at the win, and it will always be a special memory for me, as he went home to be with the Lord two months later.

Now, whenever I watch sports, I think of how obedience is the foundation for how a team works and plays together. If a player chooses to do his own thing, the coach will pull him out of the game for not obeying, and there is often a fine to pay. Mom and Dad, it works the same way for your child's success in life. We encourage you to train your child to obey like Samuel did when his name was called.

Are you ready to get started? In the next few chapters, we will show you how to teach your children to behave.

As parents of seven children, ages one to thirteen years, we can honestly say that we don't know where we would be today if we hadn't had this teaching on obedience training. While the biblical background gives us the significance of the training and the reason for it, the practicality of this instruction on obedience has made it easy to understand and has given us tremendous confidence in our parenting. So many behavioral issues that other parents deal with aren't issues for us because we deal with things at the obedience level. People stop us all the time, amazed at how well our children behave. They can tell their behavior is not forced. It is just the way they are. Our home is a happy place because of the biblical obedience teaching presented here.

—Kevin and Julie, Iowa

"Sons are a heritage from the Lord,
children are a reward from him.
Like arrows in the hands of a warrior
are sons born in one's youth."
Psalm 127:3

CHAPTER 2

WHAT OBEDIENCE IS

Little League baseball is a favorite activity of preteen boys, and I (Joey) was no exception. It was toward the end of the season, and when I was up for bat in a game, I thought the pitch was way outside the strike zone. The umpire called it strike three, and I was out. Three similar calls were made on me, and I let the umpire and all my teammates know how bad I thought the calls were. Those pitches were balls. Everyone but the umpire knew they were balls, and I should have made it to base and possibly been able to score runs for my team.

Because I was the starting third baseman for the team, everyone was surprised when Coach put me on the bench for the entire game the next time we played, especially since my dad was the assistant coach. Tired of listening to my complaining, my dad told me I didn't have the right to challenge the umpire. He said my attitude was the reason I was not chosen to be on the league's coveted all-star team. To say I was disappointed would be an understatement. Looking back on it, I can see how my dad helped me learn to be respectful and to accept when I was not in control.

Parents, if necessary, are you willing to pull your child out of the game of life to get his heart to the point of obedience?

Obedience Has Four Parts

After reading the last chapter, you might be wondering how you can get your children to come when you call their name when they won't even make their beds unless you threaten them with their lives.

The best thing that happened to us when we went to the parenting conference where we first heard this teaching was being invited to homes for meals. At the first home we went to, the mother called her daughter, who was around eight years old.

The girl said, "Yes, Mom." And she went to where her mother stood.

Her mother asked, "Please put the silverware on the table?"

She responded, "Yes, Mom, I will be glad to."

This was impressive! The mother called her son next, who was about six years old.

He went to her immediately, saying, "Yes, Mom," as he walked.

His mom asked, "Please tell your dad that I would like to speak to him."

The boy said, "Yes, Mom, I will go find Dad and let him know you want to talk to him."

This was amazing! I (Carla) asked this mom what she, wanting to impress us, bribed her kids with. She told me they had been using the principles we were learning at the conference for a few years and for her children to respond when their name was called was a firmly ingrained habit. After seeing this, we were ready to learn more about obedience training.

***

Before he was adept at walking, Michael loved to roam about the living room in his little walker. He would pull things off the shelves of the open bookcase. We removed the things that were precious to us and left the rest, knowing he needed to learn not to touch.

Michael would take one of his father's record albums and flip it across the room like a Frisbee, shrieking with delight. I tried distracting him and giving him something else to do to no avail. As soon as I put him in the walker, he headed straight for the bookcase.

I swatted his hand when he touched the albums so many times it was beet red. In tears, I called Joey home from church where he served as a youth pastor. I told him he was going to get to stay home and train his son, and I would go back to work. Joey did stay home that afternoon to show me parenting was not difficult, but by dinner, he was singing a different tune. Dad stuck to his guns, yet Michael did not give in. We were confident we had the strongest-willed child in the universe!

We were introduced to the *Growing Kids God's Way* parenting curriculum[1] during the conference we attended that we mentioned in the first chapter. I (Carla) was relieved to have a parenting plan based on biblical principles that would work for our strong-minded son. Michael was in second grade at the time, and the girls were four and two years old.

Without this teaching, we often wonder if we would have the beautiful relationships we now have with our three adult children. It brings a smile to our hearts when we watch our son, now a father himself, work with his strong-minded young son to teach him the meaning of the word "No."

There are four parts to obedience: obeying immediately, completely, no challenging and no complaining. We will look at these one at a time.

Obeying Immediately

When God called Samuel's name, He got an immediate response, even though Samuel thought Eli was calling him. Do you expect to get a response when you call your child's name? Does he respond right away or whenever he feels like it? We know parents want to hear from their child right away. Can you see how training your child to come to you immediately when you call his name fits into the obedience process?

The first part of training your kids to obey is teaching them to come to you immediately when you call their name with a positive response. Before we heard this teaching, we would call our children's names and tell them what we wanted them to do without taking a breath. It was difficult to learn to say their name and wait for a response.

Friends of ours were working on this at the same time we were. Call waiting was a big thing with the phone service at the time. Our friend shared with us that he told himself to think of "call waiting" when he called his kids so he would stop after he said their names. After that, every time we called one of our children's name, we tried to mentally think, "Call and wait." It did help.

A Positive Response

Some of you might be so happy at the thought that your children would come to you at the call of their names that you might think we are pushing it a bit by expecting a positive verbal response.

Let's put it another way. You call your son's name, wait for his response, and hear, "What!!" What are the chances he will do what you are getting ready to tell him to do if he already has a bad attitude?

Regardless of what your children might think, "Whatever … Yeah … What do you want?" or the like are not positive verbal responses.

In military families or those who live in the southern United States, a positive verbal response might be "Yes, ma'am/sir." For the rest of us, "Yes, Mom/Dad" will do. For older children (middle school and above), "Yes" is enough. For children in second grade and below, "Yes, Mommy, I'm coming" gets them moving toward you.

If you don't get a positive verbal response, your child's attitude will continue to deteriorate after you give him your instruction. What is the point of letting it get that far out of control?

Parental Intervention

When your child's attitude is out of control, it is very difficult to bring it back under control. Rare is the child who can bring it back without parental intervention. When we ask parents what "parental intervention" looks like for them, we often hear they yell at their children, threaten them, bribe them, ground them, and so forth.

For us, parental intervention meant our children would get one warning. If they did not bring themselves under control or repeated the misbehavior, they were told to sit to calm down and get self-control. They were not allowed to get up from the chair until they were ready to apologize. After they apologized, they received a consequence.

Telling your child to go and sit to get self-control is not a consequence. It gives him the chance to think about what he is doing and to get ready to apologize. It gives you both a chance to calm down.

Sitting or No Sitting

When we are teaching before a live audience, the question we always get at this point is what to do if your child won't sit or won't stay in the chair. These are our recommendations if your child will not go to his spot (have one designated for him) to sit:

- Leave him alone until he calms down.

- Once you see he is calm, call him again.

- Since he is calm, he should come to you.

- When he does, ask him if he is ready to apologize for not coming to you the appropriate way the first time you called him.

- If he is ready, hear his apology and then tell him he gets a consequence for not coming and for not sitting when he was instructed to.

- If he isn't ready to apologize, send him back to his chair to sit some more.

We will talk more about consequences later.

When you first start to do this, you may be sending him back to the chair to sit for the rest of the day, but when he realizes you are not going to give in and he isn't doing anything fun, he will go sit. When you start to work on the obedience process, it is best to clear your schedule for a few days so you can give this training your full attention.

It Looks Like This

So what does obeying immediately look like? It shouldn't matter what a child is doing. When his name is called, he should respond in this way. [2] I (Carla) want my daughter, Amy to pick up her toys before lunch.

"Amy!"

"Yes, Mommy, I'm coming!" Amy said as she comes to me.

"Thank you for coming when I called your name. Please pick up your toys. It is time for lunch," I told her.

"Yes, Mommy, I will pick up my toys now," Amy said.

***

The steps to take when you are training your child to come to you immediately are as follows. Please keep in mind that this is age-appropriate, and the general age for the following is four years and above, although we have seen many three year olds who have been able to follow through with these guidelines as well.

1. Call your child's name and wait for his response.

2. Your child is to get up immediately, and come to you, saying "Yes Mommy (Daddy) I'm coming.

3. You praise him for coming when he was called, and tell him why you called him.

4. Your child gives another positive verbal response, indicating he intends to comply.

5. Your child goes to do what you have asked right away.

When a child in fifth grade and up responds to you this way by habit, and you are sure he will remember the instruction, you can tell him he can wait until a later time to fulfill it.

For example, if your ten-year-old is doing her homework, you could say, "When you get your homework done, would you please set the table for dinner?" This brings balance to obeying immediately.

Obeying Completely

To obey completely is the second part of the obedience training process. It means a child will:

- Do what he is being asked to do

- Do it the way it is supposed to be done

- Do it without having to be told to go and do it again because he didn't do it right the first time

Parents often ask us if this is a dream. We know it can be done because we have seen it in our own family as well as in families all over the world.

When training a child to do a task completely, call his name, wait for his response and tell him what you want him to do. When he responds he will do the task, ask him to come tell you when he is done. This way you can go check and see if he has done it completely.

For a child to complete a task correctly, he would have to first know how it is supposed to be done. When our kids started helping in the kitchen, one of the first tasks they were given to do was empty the plastic pieces out of the dishwasher. When they were old enough to complete this chore, they were each carefully shown how to do this task in a way that would please me (Carla).

I will admit to being rather persnickety about the way this task was accomplished. I wanted to find the containers neatly stacked in the cupboard and the lids kept in the bin next to them. One morning, upon opening the cabinet door where the plastic containers were stored, the containers and lids fell all over the floor.

Michael was sitting at the table eating breakfast, so I asked him, "Whose job is it to empty the plastic containers?"

He told me, "Its Amy's job."

I called Amy's name in a tone that let her know she was in trouble.

As she came down the stairs, Michael calmly said, "Have you ever showed her how you want the stuff to be put in the cabinet?" I still have no idea what made him think of this.

If Amy had been given this task, she would have been shown how to do it. Or so I thought. Hard as I tried, I could not remember telling her this was now her job. When Amy came into the kitchen, I asked her if she had ever been shown how to put the plastic containers away.

She said, "No. No one has ever shown me how to do it."

I asked, "When did you get the job?"

She told me Briana (whose job it had been) told her it was time for Amy to take it over.

I asked her, "Do you want to keep the job?" I would gladly give it back to Briana.

Amy said, "I do want to keep it."

I showed her how it was to be done.

***

It was hard for Joey and I to understand why our kids would have to do a job again and again because they didn't do it the way they knew it was supposed to be done the first time they worked on it. We were consistent with giving consequences. We finally decided to approach this a different way.

When Michael was old enough to mow the lawn, I (Joey) took him aside and told him that he would get paid what the teens who mowed our lawn the previous summer had received in payment. He would get paid at the end of the each month, under the following requirements.

If Michael had to be reminded once to mow during a month, had to do it over because he did not do it correctly, or whined or complained about mowing, he would still mow the lawn every week, he just wouldn't get paid for it that month. On his third summer of mowing, Michael told us at dinner one night that he intended to get paid every month that summer. And he did.

A couple summers ago, I (Joey) asked a teenager if he wanted to mow our lawn all summer. He did it a couple times and didn't show up one week. When I called him, he said he didn't need any money right then so he wasn't going to mow the lawn that week. Needless to say, mowing our lawn became a thing of the past for this young man, and once again, I was thankful I had the insight to use the lawn to teach Michael how to do a job completely with a good attitude.

When your children come to the one in authority who is calling their name immediately and do what is asked of them completely, these are the *action* sides of obedience. They both require your child's body to move. We are ready to move on to the two parts that make up the *attitude* side of obedience.

No Challenging

When your child challenges you, he is saying you do not have the right to tell him what to do. He is telling you he is in control, and you do not have authority in his life.

These children belong to you. This gives you the right to tell them what to do. It gives you the responsibility of authority, and parents need to learn how to use this authority wisely.

When your children are challenging you, whether they are three, ten, or sixteen years of age, you need to rise to the challenge they are presenting to you. You do not need a houseful of little roosters running around butting heads with each other.

Please do not think you can talk them through it, negotiate with them, get into a debate, or argue with them. This rarely works, no matter what age your children are. You will gain nothing except a headache, a lost temper, and a power struggle.

Once your child starts talking to you when he should have said "Yes, Mom/Dad," send him to sit until he has self-control and is ready to apologize. When he sits, he is not to talk or get out of the chair until he is ready to apologize.

After your child apologizes, ask him if he is ready to hear the instruction you were going to give. If not, send him to sit until he is.

If parents choose not to deal with a challenge to their authority, this child will continue to take control of the family, and all who reside in this home will be miserable.

No Complaining

A complaining child is not saying you don't have the right to tell him what to do. He is telling you that he doesn't feel like doing it. The difference between a complaining child and a challenging child is huge. Again, look at the motivation behind the attitude. The most common form of complaining is whining.

When your child whines, it is best to catch it early so it does not get out of control. When whining gets out of control, it can escalate to the point where it turns into a challenging tantrum. Parents can avoid this by stopping the whining early on.

When your child whines, send him to sit until he gets self-control and is willing to apologize for his complaining attitude. After he apologizes, he should tell you he is willing to complete the task you assigned him with no more whining. If one of our children was sent to sit for whining more than one time in a morning or afternoon, he would get a consequence after he apologized and completed the task.

Our daughter Briana was a whiner when she was young. She asked me (Carla) once why I hated whining so much. She thought it was a lot nicer way of showing me she didn't want to do what I had instructed her to do than the tantrums her brother indulged in.

She was surprised to learn we already knew she didn't want to complete a task before we assigned it to her. I told her there was no need to whine, pout, sulk, or give us the silent treatment anymore because doing these things would only get her in worse trouble.

Action vs. Attitude

Parents are often content to get the action side of obedience and let the attitude side slide. Does it matter what their attitude is as long as they do what they have been instructed to do?

You are training your children to become adults one day. Do you think their future employers will think it is acceptable to just get the job done, no matter how bad their attitude is while doing it?

One way parents let the attitude side of obedience slide is to give consequences for an action that was not completed or was done incorrectly and lecture for a bad attitude. Your home is the training laboratory for your child to have an attitude adjustment. Your child's overall attitude directly reflects what you do or do not allow in your home.

Apologies are Important

Have you noticed that a child needs to apologize to get up from sitting when he is in trouble? We used to tell our kids that their apology was the gate they had to open to get out of the chair. It is crucial a child five years of age and up admits he was wrong in what he did while he is apologizing. If he never admits he was wrong, he will not see the need to change the offending behavior. When a child says, "I'm sorry," he is not admitting he was wrong. He is just admitting he is sorry he got caught.

Apologizing looks like this. A child needs to:

1. Admit he was wrong, and tell what he did that was wrong. To say, "I didn't obey," is not good enough. It is too generic. He needs to state what his disobedience looked like.

2. Tell why it was wrong.

3. Ask for forgiveness, which is making the relationship right with the one he offended.

4. Tell what he will do to make it right, such as go and do what he was asked with a good attitude, or admit he needs to apologize to his siblings if he has offended them.

5. Accept the consequence.

If a child is truly apologetic, he will calmly accept the consequence. This is why we recommend you give the consequence to your child after he apologizes. Apologizing is a key part of training children to obedience. To apologize correctly takes a humble spirit. Kids behave when they are humble, and they are pleasant to be around.

One Thing at a Time

Is this beginning to sound like a daunting task, to train your children to these four parts of obedience? It should! But there is a way to avoid becoming overwhelmed or frustrated in this process. We cannot encourage you enough to work on one thing at a time. There is no way you can train your children in all four parts of obedience at the same time because you won't be consistent and you will be giving too many consequences to your children. How do you work on one thing at a time?

- Work with your children to come when you call their name immediately with a positive verbal response.

- Sit your children down and role-play with them. Both parents should be involved in this so the kids can see they agree this is what will happen in the family.

- The parents should role-play first with one calling the other's name and the one being called giving a positive verbal response.

- The parents practice with the kids.

Give your kids a week to work on remembering to come when you call their names with a positive verbal response.

You will only give a consequence for this one part of the obedience process. Reminders will do for not completing the task. You can let the complaining attitude go for now. This is how you work on one thing at a time.

With children less than eight years of age, when you start to work on this, call their name frequently throughout the day. Praise them when they come to you with a positive verbal response. With children less than three years of age, pat your thigh and tell them to come to Mommy or Daddy. Patting your thigh gives them a destination to come to.

After you are sure they understand what you are asking them to do, you will need to start giving consequences when they choose not to come to you or don't give a positive verbal response.

When to Move On

Once your children are coming immediately when you call their names and are giving you a positive verbal response so often that you are not giving them very many consequences for this, start working on seeing they complete their tasks the way you have instructed them to.

When you start to work on getting them to do the assigned task completely, don't give up working on getting them to come to you immediately. You surely don't want to lose the ground you have already gained while you are tackling a new part of training your child to obedience.

When your child comes to the call of his name immediately and fulfills the instruction completely, and you no longer are giving him very many consequences for either of these, you can start working on your child's challenging attitude.

Some of this should have diminished just by getting the action parts of obedience to a high standard. If your child still has to sit to get his attitude under control before you have even given the instruction, it is time to start giving consequences for his challenging attitude.

When your child comes without challenging you immediately and follows through with the instruction completely, you can move on to nipping the whining (no complaining) in the bud. You would proceed in the same way we have described above.[3]

Single Parents Can Do It Too

Single parents, don't despair! If your parents live nearby and you have a good relationship with them, share with them what you want to do to train your children to obey and ask them if they will help you by coming alongside you and following your example.

If you have a good relationship with your ex-spouse, ask him (or her) to go out for coffee and have this conversation with him. If your ex-spouse is not open to what you share, don't think there is no use in trying to train your children in obedience.

Higher Standards Are Okay

Do you remember when you were in middle school, high school, or college? You had different classes with different teachers in different rooms. When you were in their room, each teacher had different standards and expectations, what he would put up with and how he would grade. Did you have any problem adjusting to their different standards? Think of your children's other parent in the same way.

You and your ex-spouse each have different standards and expectations of what you will and won't put up with when your child is with you. Single parents often feel they can't have a higher expectation of obedience than their ex-spouse does.

Just as you were able to adjust to going to different classrooms knowing what the teacher in each room expected, your children will be able to go back and forth between the homes of you and your ex-spouse, knowing what is expected of them once they drive up to each home.

Single parents, please don't think your children won't love you if you hold higher standards in your home than your ex-spouse does. They will love you because they know you unconditionally love them and will always be there for them.

My (Carla's) parents separated when I was in high school. When my sisters and I spent time with my father, who lived a few hours away from us, he would buy us nice things as a way to show us he loved us. We greedily accepted his gifts.

When we returned home, our mother did not let up on her stricter rules and boundaries. My sisters and I have all been married for more than thirty years. Each of us are strong Christians and have good marriages and families. To a large degree, this is because of the love and spiritual wisdom of my mother.

A single mom attended one of the first parenting classes we led. She struggled through the class, and we weren't sure how well she was going to apply the teaching. We saw her several times around town over the years, and she would always remind us she was still working on getting her children to obey.

It has been over fifteen years now since she first took that class with us. We recently saw her, and she told us her son is now a father and he is working on training his son in obedience. For teachers, it doesn't get better than this.

We want to encourage single parents who are thinking of remarrying to get on the same parenting page with your potential spouse before you decide to marry. This is especially critical if this person is a parent as well. When a couple is not on the same parenting page, many blended families will self-destruct before they barely get started.

You can train your children to the same standard as a two-parent household. Please don't ever assume it won't work out.

As parents of four teenagers, we are now enjoying a fun-filled, fast-paced home where there is harmony and joy. We realize, though, that we would be dealing with frustration and disappointment if we had not understood how critical obedience is, especially in their younger years. When the kids were small, we focused on teaching them to obey us immediately and completely, without challenge and without complaining. We were not afraid to provide consequences when they didn't obey. Because they learned to obey when they were young, we were able to successfully train them in character and moral traits, and as they grew and matured, this led to us having a strong relationship with them now, which we are very thankful for.

—Luke and Luona, New York

"Train up a child in the way he should go;
and when he is old he will not turn from it."
Proverbs 22:6

CHAPTER 3

THE PARENTING TOOLBOX

Visitors to the Ozark Mountains in Missouri and Arkansas will find little shops along the way that sell handmade, beautifully crafted furniture. Examining the pieces, one can only imagine the work that went into taking a piece of wood and working with it to create quality furniture.

I (Joey) like to do woodworking projects. I still get a smile on my face when I think about the cedar-lined hope chests I made for both of our daughters and our daughter-in-law. Once the carving, sanding, staining, gluing, and varnishing are finished, the result is beautiful and will stand the test of time. It takes a lot of tools to fix and create projects out of wood. Wanting to find a tool quickly when I need it, I keep the tools in a toolbox just for them.

I use a clamp when gluing together pieces of wood. Choosing what size clamp to use takes thought. The biggest clamp can glue boards up to six feet wide but can become cumbersome to use and difficult to tighten properly. If I grab the eight-inch clamp and the clamp needs to have a twelve-inch opening, it won't work either. The same thing is true for the tools you need to reach for when parenting your children. You need to use the right tool for the right situation for the right child.

Training your children is like crafting fine furniture. It takes years of carving, shaping, molding, and sanding to get the finished product you will send into the world one day. Young adults who understand the importance of both obedience and submission and have hearts that have been trained in godly character are emotional, mental and spiritual treasures that will leap ahead of others their age.

Do you know you have a parenting toolbox available for your use? We will share several tools that will assist you with your parenting, starting with creating routine in your day.

The Tool of Routine

Michele let out a deep sigh as she watched two-year-old Alisha and four-year-old Erin fight over which DVD to watch. Michele had run errands earlier with the kids, stopped for a late lunch, and battled over naps … and now this. Her husband would be coming home to a messy house, cranky children, an exhausted wife, and leftover spaghetti. Michele bent over to pick up a toy when she felt a sharp kick. How would she ever handle another baby? Did all moms feel this way?

It doesn't take young moms long to realize that nothing is predictable with young children, and they cannot count on anything in their day. Every day can be disorganized, hectic, and tiring. There is no sense of accomplishment, except Mom made it to bed at the end of the day and all the kids were still alive.

Parenting toddlers and preschoolers can seem to last forever. But there is something that will bring peace back to your home.

Our daughter Briana was born with respiratory problems and was on breathing treatments every four hours around the clock, taking all of my (Carla's) time and energy. Joey was working in youth ministry, overseeing the middle school, high school, and college youth groups at our large church.

Michael, almost five years old, was left to do what he wanted as long as he didn't break anything or hurt himself. Thankfully, we had a large fenced-in backyard, and the Southern California sunshine allowed him to play there almost every day.

Life wasn't easy. I (Carla) worried constantly about Briana's health, knew Michael wasn't getting enough attention, and wanted to be involved in the youth ministry with Joey.

My mom, who lived in another state, came for a visit. Although she was not one to interfere with the decisions her adult children made, it did not take long for her to see I needed help. She started working to get the kids on a routine.

She worked with me to get Michael and Briana their meals at the same time each day, give Michael a rest time every day—which he was willing to do when Grandma gave him one toy to play with and assured him he didn't have to sleep, and get the kids to bed at the same time each night. She showed me how to plan things for Michael to do that would keep him occupied during Briana's thirty minute breathing treatments.

I could see good results by the time she left, and I was especially encouraged to see Michael's behavior improve.

Parents, including me, are often amazed to see how adding routine to their child's day eliminates ther need for a lot of corrective discipline. The more routine you add to your child's day, the more discipline you will be able to subtract from it. A good routine enhances good organization of time and helps mom achieve her personal goals.[1]

Does Structure Work Against Your Grain?

Many mothers are not inclined toward structure. I (Carla) fell into this camp. When my mom talked to me about getting the kids on a routine, I wondered if it was even feasible for me to consider. If you are thinking this too, don't give up before you even get started.

Because opposites do attract, Joey lives by lists. He is discouraged when he doesn't get to cross off everything on his to-do list every day.

For years, at Christmas and on my birthday, Joey would give me day planners, briefcases, notebooks and such, attempting to organize my life. I would remind him my calendar and Post-it notes worked just fine for me, and in response, I would get a look that told me he was never going to agree with me on this. I have, however, having lived with him all these years, learned that there are positives to keeping oneself on a routine.

What Routine Looks Like

Routine brings order to a child's day, and order brings predictability, which gives a child security. Children function much better when they feel secure. So what does a routine for two- and three-year-old children look like?

For a toddler, make a list of activities he can do while in a playpen, sitting in the high chair, or other places he can be contained without direct supervision. When you need to give your undivided attention elsewhere, put your toddler in one of these places and give him one of the activities on the list you made to do.

Playpen Time

We encourage you to consider training your child to playpen time. To start playpen time with babies and children up to two years of age, get a portable kitchen timer you can put by the playpen, but where your child can't reach it.

If you put your child in the playpen and he cries the whole time until you go and get him, what are you teaching him? He thinks you will come if he cries hard enough and long enough. Using a timer avoids this dilemma. He quickly learns you will come when the bell goes off and not before.

Start with small increments of time, such as three minutes. After you have set the timer, go to a place where your child can't see you. The goal of playpen time is to teach your child to entertain himself.

If he throws his toys outside his playpen or cries the entire time, try not to give in to the urge to give them back to him or go and cuddle with him. If you do, you will be starting a game he will gladly play until the timer goes off, as he will cry and throw his toys overboard the minute you leave the room again. This is the reason it is best to start with three minutes. Both you and your child can endure that amount of time.

Have playpen time two times a day when your child is not tired. When he sits and plays without crying for the entire three minutes for five consecutive days, set the timer for five minutes. When he sits and plays without crying for five minutes for five days, set the timer for seven minutes. You can keep increasing the time until your child will sit and play for thirty minutes.

On a visit to see our eighteen-month old grandson, his Papa (Joey) had been keeping him busily entertained for quite a while. Hudson's mom decided he needed some quiet time and put him in the playpen for playpen time. He played with the toys she gave him for a while. A thud was heard, and we all knew a toy had been pitched over the side of the playpen. It was soon followed by another thud. Now both toys he had been given to play with were gone.

Hudson let out a shriek. Michael went to the room he was in and pointed to the timer and quickly left. Hudson happily talked to himself until the timer went off, at which time he started clapping because he knew his "Papa time" would begin anew.

Think about it. What chore can you do in five minutes? What about seven, ten, or fifteen minutes? You can start the laundry, load the dishwasher, and make your bed in a few minutes of uninterrupted time. Once your child will play in the playpen without crying, you have this time to get things done.

You can take the playpen and have playpen time at Grandma's or outside when you need to work in the yard. Playpen time is a blessing to parents, especially busy mothers.

Routine for Preschoolers

Make a list of the activities your preschool child will do without supervision, such as playing with blocks, cars, or dolls, sitting at the table coloring a picture, or working puzzles. Next to the activity, write down how many minutes your preschooler will be occupied with this activity before getting bored.

If you have older children who don't require supervision, write down the activities they each would be willing to do with your preschooler that would take fifteen minutes, such as reading books or playing a game. If an older sibling knows you won't ask for more than fifteen minutes or so of his time, he will likely cooperate with a good attitude when you ask him to do something with his younger sibling.

Now, write down a list of activities you can do with your preschooler that will take fifteen minutes per activity, such as letting them "read" a book to you, playing hairdresser with your daughter, or tickling your son on his bed.

Before you go to bed each night, write down the things that you need to get accomplished the next day. Next to the activities you have just written down that require your attention elsewhere, working off the lists of activities your young child can do without being supervised or with a sibling, slot them in during these times.

Alternate these times with an activity you can do with your child. If you need to run an errand (knowing that toddlers and preschoolers are not going to endure a long list of errands without misbehaving), work that in when your child is fresh and alert. First thing in the morning or after naps work best.

Write down something Daddy can do with your young child when he gets home, such as taking the child for a walk around the block or building a boat or castle with the child's blocks. Even fifteen minutes of uninterrupted time will go a long way with young children, and Dad will appreciate not having to think of something to do with his children himself after a long day at work.

What About Working Moms?

It doesn't matter if Mom stays at home with her children or works—a routine is still a great tool to have in her toolbox. It is best if Mom can find child care that will stick to a routine.

Most day care centers do. It is more difficult to get a child care worker who will come to your home to stick to one. If this is the case, you can still have a routine for the time you and your spouse are with the kids.

Routine Works for Children of All Ages

Adults function better if they eat and sleep at the same time each day. In the same way, children of all ages do better with a routine. Too much free time leads to chaos, and someone often gets hurt if siblings are together without supervision for long periods of time.

For children in the elementary school grades, come up with a routine for them for the time before and after school. Make a list of the activities that need to be done during these times, including chores and Bible time. Write down how much time each activity will take to accomplish.

Put all your children's lists before you on the kitchen table. Make a list for each of them of the order and times they will get these activities done and how much time they have to do them. If your children can't be in the bathroom brushing their teeth at the same time without fighting with each other, make sure they are not in there together. This avoids a lot of tension in the morning from squabbling siblings.

When you get used to making the routines, it is often easier to make them by the week. Older children can make their own routines. Have them write down their routines for the next day each night before they go to bed. Encourage your older kids to show you their next day's routine each night so you can double-check and see if they left out anything you know they need to get done. Moms will not believe how much this tool will bring peace and calm to their homes. [2]

The Tool of Discipline

When children misbehave, they need to be disciplined. Interestingly enough, the word "discipline" means *"To teach or instruct; training that corrects, molds, strengthens or perfects; control gained by enforcing obedience."*[3] The Iowa Department of Human Services describes discipline in their Foster Parent Handbook:

> *To discipline is to teach or instruct. Through discipline, you teach the child responsible behavior. Before providing discipline, ask yourself, "What do I want this child to learn and how can I best teach this child?" The foster parent who is a disciplinarian is really a teacher, a guide, and a counselor who helps the child learn. Take opportunities to get additional training or do additional reading on discipline to meet the child's needs. As you increase your knowledge and skills, you will find that addressing challenging behavior is less stressful and you will feel more in control of the situation.*[4]

This is excellent advice for all parents. Training your children in obedience is a discipline. By reading this book you hold in your hands, you are getting additional knowledge and skills for teaching and training your children effectively, and we have already talked about your need to be in control of the family.

Another way to look at discipline is to see it as discipleship. As Christians, we are called to make disciples (Matthew 28:19-20). To disciple someone is to be a mentor to him in right behavior and Godly living. There is not greater responsibility one has as a parent than to teach God's values to your children.

No Pain, No Gain

Corrective discipline includes giving consequences. No parent wants to cause his child pain. This is the problem with giving consequences. Yet God created pain for a reason. When you feel pain in your body, you seek medical attention to see what is wrong. When you feel pain in your wallet, you cut back on your spending.

A sign on the wall at the gym where we work out says, "No Pain, No Gain." Unfortunately, this is true for all of us. Pain has a place in life. For children, one of these places is to motivate them to obey in both action and attitude. Pain serves to teach children to do what they are supposed to do.

For consequences to be effective, they must be painful, and they must be given consistently. If you are unwilling to give your child consequences that will cause him enough pain to motivate him to behave, how will he learn to do so? You can talk to him, lecture him, bribe him, and beg him to behave all you want, but eventually, you will learn these will only produce quick fixes, if any at all.

When someone joins the military, he goes to boot camp. We lived near a large military base in Southern California when we were first married, and several men in our church were military men.

Being the curious sort, Joey asked one of these men, a drill sergeant, what his role was during boot camp.

This man said, "I teach the recruits to do what they are told to do when they are told to do it."

Joey responded by telling this officer he thought the new recruits should have learned that before they joined the military.

"Nowadays," the sergeant replied, "the recruits think they can tell us to do something a different way, or they want to discuss whether it really needs to be done, or they tell us they don't agree with what we are telling them to do, so they refuse to comply.

When I am standing with these kids facing an enemy's attack and I tell them to fire, they don't get to take the time to question my order. They will immediately pick up their weapon and fire, or the cost of not doing what I told them to do when I told them to do it could very well be theirs and others' lives."

The military understands obedience cannot be taught when the soldiers are standing on the battlefield. The officers in charge at boot camp know that everything soldiers need to learn to prepare for the possibility of battle depends on their level of obedience. Boot camp ensures all soldiers in the squadron are on the same obedience page.

Your home is your child's boot camp. If you don't teach your children to be obedient when they are growing up, you are sending them into adulthood with a severe disability. They will have to learn to obey at the command of someone in authority who doesn't have a personal interest in them.

God does not expect us to do something we are not capable of doing. Therefore, it is possible for every human being, including your children, to be obedient. *"Children obey your parents in the Lord for this is right"* (Ephesians 6:1) is very clear. It does not say, "Unless you are in a good mood, have nothing else to do, or you feel like it." This verse says, despite any circumstance, children are to obey.

Colossians 3:20 says, *"Children, obey your parents in everything."* There's no "I forgot" or negotiating, debating, arguing, whining, or complaining. There are no excuses and no exceptions.

Can children forget? There is a difference between a child forgetting on occasion and forgetting every day as an excuse to get out of following through with his responsibilities. "In everything" does not leave *anything* to one's imagination.

The Tools of Consequence

Consequences are positive tools for parents to use because they motivate children to do what is right. Parents commonly use grounding as a consequence. When a child is grounded, he loses the privilege of doing something he likes to do.

Michael was being irresponsible on a daily basis. He was twelve years old, and it was getting to the point where we could not count on him to get his stuff done. We tried grounding him, although we already knew it didn't work.

Parents think the loss of the computer for the rest of the day is sufficient motivation for their child to choose to obey the next time they call his name or he needs to get his chores done. Really? Kids have way too much stuff for the loss of one thing to break them, especially when well-meaning parents don't take away things for enough time to make a difference to their child.

The problem with grounding is the child is just serving his time, much like a criminal in prison. I (Carla) did an internship while in college in juvenile probation. I worked for a time in a large juvenile facility in Southern California. When their release date drew near, the kids would start talking about returning to the same activities that landed them in detention in the first place. Working in juvenile probation as a field officer taught me the same thing. Detention was not a sufficient deterrent for teens to change bad habits.

Not being able to offer them the promise of a relationship with Jesus Christ made me feel hopeless, so I knew I would not pursue this as a full-time career upon graduation. I married a youth pastor instead and often felt my time as a field officer in juvenile probation was a good thing to have under my belt for my role in youth ministry!

When kids are serving time, whether in juvenile hall or being grounded at home, they just wait for the time to be up. What has motivated them to change their behavior? Do your children soon return to the behaviors that got them grounded in the first place? We are certain they do.

At one time, Michael was getting into trouble at school because he was not getting his homework done. Since he was getting all A's on his report card, he didn't see why he needed to do homework as he already knew and understood the assignments.

He was in the habit of flipping on the television when he got home from school. We took the television away for a week, and he played video games when he got home instead. We took away the video games on top of the television. He went outside and rode his bike, so we took that away as well.

After a period of time, it was getting complicated remembering what we had taken away and for how long because all the time periods overlapped. This is another reason grounding doesn't work. We stumbled on a better way.

No More Grounding

We learned not to set a time limit when we took away the privilege of something. We would tell our kids they lost the freedom of whatever we took away and asked them what they had to do to get that freedom back. When it comes to consequences, this should be your golden rule:

Take away what they are misusing.

You will not believe what a difference this will make.

When you take away the privilege of what your child has misused, don't give him a time limit.

He will ask, "For how long?"

Your answer should sound like this, "I don't know. What do you think I need to see before you can get it back?" Trust us. You will throw your child for a loop when you do this.

"I have to do something to get it back?" your bewildered child will whine.

Frankly, it is easier for your children to just serve the time given when grounded or sitting in a time-out. By not giving them a time limit, you are putting the burden of their disobedient action back on them. The ball is back in their court.

When we started doing this with our son (who was in middle school at the time) he would say, "You would think I need to get my homework done before I can have the freedom to watch television again."

We told him, "It doesn't matter what we think. What do you think you need to do?"

Mom and Dad, don't let your child make his rebellion about you. It is about him. He knows why he lost the freedom of something important to him.

One of our daughters would not pick up her dirty clothes after she took them off. I (Carla) would confiscate them and put her clothes in a laundry basket in my bedroom when I found them on Briana's bedroom or bathroom floor. When Briana was out of all her favorite clothes, she offered to wash them for me. She was in fifth grade, and how she looked was becoming increasingly important to her.

"Briana, getting your clothes washed is not the problem. I can do them when I do the laundry. What do you think the problem is?"

"You and Dad are mad because I keep forgetting to pick my clothes up," Briana replied.

"No, that's not the problem either," I told her.

Briana was told to go and sit until she was willing to discuss the problem. After a time she came to me and I could tell by the look on her face she was ready to talk.

"I know what the problem is," Briana said. "I am choosing not to remember to pick my clothes up and put them away."

She admitted it was not important to her to remember to check and see that she had picked them up. We asked her what it was going to take for picking up her clothes to become important to her. She wanted her favorite clothes back, so she started picking up her clothes and putting them in the dirty clothes basket in her room. I wanted this to become a habit, so she didn't get her favorite clothes back for two long weeks.

Neither of our daughters would turn off the bathroom light when they left that room. Joey took away the privilege of having a light in the bathroom. It was comical to watch them figure out how to overcome this difficulty. They took their showers at night because they could not seem to shower in the morning and get started with school on time. They weren't allowed to use candles. They tried flashlights. After a couple days of futile attempts to get light, they made sure they turned out the lights whenever they left any room.

When our kids were harsh in their tone, they lost the freedom to speak. When our daughter Amy was six years old, she would run out of the house when we were going somewhere to get her favorite seat in the van. She didn't care who she pushed or shoved on her way. She lost the freedom of getting in the vehicle until all others were seated.

We know a family who has four boys. They were homeschooling, and Mom was frustrated with all the pushing, shoving, and hitting that occurred each day. She took away the freedom of using their hands, which they had to keep in the pockets of their jeans, yet they still had to get their chores and school done that day. When the boys went to bed that night, they begged their mom to give the freedom of their hands back.

Another family told us of the time one of their daughters would not help her siblings when asked. When her sister had to get to an appointment and this child refused to help her get a chore done, she gained the responsibility of doing all of her sister's chores on top of her own until she started showing a helpful spirit in the house.

Do you see how taking away what your child is misusing works? There are many creative way of giving effective consequences. This is discipline, as the dictionary and *Iowa Department of Human Services Foster Parent Handbook* describes.

When we think of training our children in character, what did they learn from these situations? By following through on a task Michael didn't like and didn't want to do, he learned to be responsible. It is easy for kids to do the things they want to do. They show responsibility when they do things they don't want to do.

Briana learned responsibility when she was faithful in taking care of her clothes. Our girls learned the importance of helping with the family budget and the environment by turning out the lights. Amy learned patience when she had to wait to get in the van.

Our friends' boys learned to show kindness, self-control, and respect for others instead of hitting each other, and our friends' daughter learned to be helpful to others whether she was asked to or not. All these children are now young adults, and they are a blessing to all who know them.

When you take away the privilege of what your children have misused and they have to earn the right to have it back, you, the parent, are no longer responsible for their irresponsibility or lack of moral virtue. They are.

As soon as kids change the behavior that got the privilege lost in the first place, they think they should get it back immediately. We made that mistake, which made taking it away totally ineffective. Remember, "No pain, no gain."

With kids in third through fifth grade, we would encourage you to start with a minimum of a week (don't tell them this or you are back to grounding them) of doing what they are supposed to do before you give that privilege back to them. Don't be discouraged if they take a long time to earn the privilege back. When they truly want it, they will.

These Consequences Occur on Their Own

Natural consequences are ones that occur on their own. You told your four-year-old many times to walk on the sidewalk. She runs, trips and falls, and gets a scraped knee. You daughter cries all the way home as you carry and comfort her. You set her on the counter in the bathroom, clean up her knee, put on antibiotic cream and a Band-Aid, kiss her, and tell her it will be okay. Getting the scraped knee was enough pain to teach her to walk next time.

Schools have consequences. If your kids are tardy enough times, they get detention. If they don't turn in their homework, they get an incomplete. If they don't get passing grades on their tests, they fail the class.

We all too often hear of parents stepping in and overriding these consequences. Why do you do this? If your kids know you will bail them out, they will keep misbehaving because they know they will get away with it.

We received an email a long time ago, saying, *"Who Says Natural Consequences Don't Work?"* It is a fun illustration of natural consequences, and although we do not know the author, we want to share it with you.

> *A middle school in Oregon was faced with a unique problem. A number of girls were beginning to use lipstick and would put it on in the bathroom. That was fine, but after they put on their lipstick, they would press their lips to the mirror, leaving dozens of little lip prints. Finally, the principal decided that something had to be done. She called all the girls to the bathroom and met them there with the maintenance man. She explained that all these lip prints were causing a major problem for the custodian who had to clean the mirrors every night. To demonstrate how difficult it was to clean the mirrors, she asked the maintenance guy to clean one of them. He took out a long-handled squeegee, dipped it into the toilet, and then cleaned the mirror. Since then, there have been no lip prints on the mirror. There are teachers… and then there are teachers.*

Enough said about consequences that occur on their own with no parental involvement required.

How Do You Use Time-Outs?

People from out of state were visiting for a week. I asked their eight-year-old daughter to take the trash from the kitchen to the garage for me. She told me in no uncertain terms she would not help me. Giving her a look, I contemplated my options.

She said, "What are you going to do? Give me a time-out for eight minutes? I will sit for eight minutes if that will make you happy, but I'm not taking the trash out. Set the timer."

Time-outs that require kids to sit for one minute for the number of years they are don't work because, like the teens in juvenile hall, kids are just serving time and not enough of it. The only way sitting for a consequence works is if kids are sitting for a period of time that is long enough to cause pain.

When kids sit for a consequence, it is the same as when they are sitting to get self-control and get ready to apologize. They should not have the freedom to talk or move about. If they are sitting for a consequence when their siblings are having fun, the pain will be greater.

When working with preschoolers, they cannot sit for a consequence unless they have learned to have self-control. One of the best ways to teach them this is to stop them when you can see they are headed for trouble, but have not yet misbehaved.

Have them sit and fold their hands, telling them to get self-control. Set a portable timer where they can see it and tell them you will come back when the bell rings to see if they are ready to get up. When they are sitting, they should not be allowed to talk or get out of the chair without your permission. During this time, encouraged your child to think about something he could do when he got up that would not get him into trouble.

Again, sitting to get self-control is not a consequence. It provides time for a child to calm down and decide on a better activity to do.

What about Spanking?

Tom and Lynne wanted their children to behave, especially in public. When discussing how to get them to obey, the conversation turned to consequences. Lynne was adamantly against spanking her children. Tom didn't have a problem with it. He reminded Lynne that he was spanked as a kid and he thought he turned out okay. What used to be a common form of correction has turned into a volatile debate among Christians.

It is a touchy thing to talk about spanking these days. However, we always get asked about it, and we know many of you will want information on it. We do believe spanking is an option when it comes to giving consequences because it is mentioned in Scripture.[5]

Spanking can be abusive, especially if the parents yell at their children while they spank them or they spank their children whenever they get angry with them.

We believe that both spouses must agree to use spanking or neither should, which is the advice we gave to Tom and Lynne. If one of you spanks and the other doesn't, your children will use you against each other. We guarantee it.

Having a degree in social work,[6] I (Carla) am passionate on this topic. If you choose to spank your kids, please pay close attention to the guidelines presented below and abide by them.

Guidelines Regarding Spanking

- **You should spank only when you are certain your child knows he has done something wrong.** If you spank your child and he does not know why he is getting the spanking, you are confusing him, and the spanking is worthless. Parents must be certain their child knows what he did wrong before they resort to spanking. Before you spank, ask your child what he did wrong and why it is wrong, so you are certain he knows.

When introducing a new behavior, work on it with your children for a week or longer before you give a consequence for it. When you can see your child is deliberately not following through with your training efforts, a consequence is appropriate.

- **You should spank for only one behavior at a time.** Spanking for only one behavior at a time keeps it under control. This means you will not spank your child any or every time you get angry or frustrated with him. Use the other consequences we have shared for other misbehaviors.

- **You should never spank when you are angry or frustrated.** You cannot control the force of the swat you are giving when you are angry. Go sit and calm down before you give your child a spanking. Take ten deep breaths. Pray and ask God for control. Never spank your children when you are having a bad day. Please don't take out your frustration with other issues in your life on your children.

- **You only need one or two swats.** Of course, like any other type of consequence, for a swat to work it has to hurt. One painful swat with a tool that leaves a sting but not a mark is all a child needs to learn a lesson. The exception to this would be lying because God considered it an abomination.[8] Our children received two swats for lying.

- **Spanking is age-appropriate.** Spanking as a consequence should diminish as your child grows and should not be used by the time your child is around ten years of age. Never spank a very young child. Remember, he has to know what he did wrong and understand why it was wrong before you can spank him.

- **You should not threaten your children with a spanking.** There is no reason to threaten your children with a spanking. If you only spank for one behavior at a time, they will know it is coming.

So does spanking have a place when determining what consequence to give? It does. Whether you choose to spank or not is up to you and your spouse. It is not a sin if you choose not to spank; nor is it a sin if you choose to spank, as long as you do so following guidelines such as the ones presented above.

We know circumstances can prevent spanking. When a single parent is in a custody battle with his or her ex-spouse, spanking is not advised, as it can easily be used against that parent. Foster parents cannot spank the children in their care.[8] If you cannot spank or choose not to, use the other consequence tools mentioned in this chapter.

> *"No discipline seems pleasant at the time,*
> *but painful. Later on, however, it produces*
> *a harvest of righteousness and peace for*
> *those who have been trained by it."*
> *Hebrews 12:11*

Tough Love

You now have a plan to lay down a firm foundation of obedience in your children. Obedient children are a joy to be around and will bring peace to your home. You will find when you are working with a consistent plan, your children are not the only ones making changes.

We had been teaching parenting classes in our church for a year. After church one morning, a couple stopped our son and asked him, "What has changed in your house since your parents started leading this class?"

I (Carla) was in an intersecting hallway where they could not see me, but I could hear them. I held my breath, wondering what Michael would say.

Without hesitation, he said, "My mom doesn't yell and scream at us anymore."

I was so very grateful to hear this. Is training your children to obedience worth the time, effort, and struggle it can take? I certainly think so.

When I (Joey) was a youth pastor, I would see the strong-willed teens in the youth groups I worked with and wondered what their adult years were going to be like. A common phrase I used when dealing with the parents of teens who wouldn't stay out of trouble was "tough love." When I suggested it was time to use tough love, I meant parents needed to clamp down on their teen and not let up until they saw necessary changes. Rarely do you hear the phrase "tough love" except when dealing with teens.

Well, let us pose this thought to you another way. Why not use tough love with your elementary school-aged children? If you consistently work to get these four parts of obedience and maintain them, you will be able to use sandpaper to round off some rough edges on your teens instead of having to use a hatchet or call in the professionals for major surgery.

These are the Right Tools

What do you want to have in your box of parenting tools you want to have handy for everyday use? These tools are:

- Routine

- Consequences: Taking away what they misused, sitting, natural consequences and spanking

• Tough Love

We will learn about more tools that go in this book later on in. So again, is training your children to obedience easy? No, it is not. Is it worth it? Absolutely!

When our three boys were young, we attended a parenting seminar taught by Joey and Carla Link. We wanted our children to behave, but we really didn't know what that looked like with kids who were two and four years of age and a baby. We were taught what obedience was and how to train our children to be obedient. We realized it was not too much to expect from young children.

It was better for the whole family when the children knew what to expect. We really appreciated how they gave so many tools and tips to help us train our children. It also gave us confidence to know what was reasonable for us to expect from our boys and what was age-appropriate.

Many other parents were at that workshop, but we wonder how many of them would say it was a life-changing event. It was for us because we applied what we had learned. There is hope for parenting, but both parents must be committed, diligent, and consistent, not only for a month or even a year, but until your child has reached adulthood.

We honestly cannot imagine what our life would be like today if we had not learned the importance of obedience all those years ago. We now have three teenage sons who are obedient and respectful young men. They are not forced to be obedient; they choose to be. We are still there to advise them as needed, but we are enjoying every minute of the journey! This is what God intended for families.

— Jeff and Dana, Missouri

"Listen my son to your father's instruction,
and do not forsake your mother's teaching.
They will be a garland to grace your head,
and a chain to adorn your neck."
Proverbs 1:8-9

CHAPTER 4

WHAT OBEDIENCE IS NOT

O ne day, we were shopping with our children. Just outside the doors of the store was a small merry-go-round. As we approached the entrance, our daughter Briana, who was four years old at the time, ran to the ride. At this time in our parenting, we kept our kids in line by counting to three. I (Joey) told Briana there was no time for the ride that morning.

She kept running, so I said loud and clear, "One!"

As she climbed on the horse, another father walked up behind me and said, "Yeah, that didn't work for me either!"

Being a family pastor, I wanted to show this father I knew what I was doing, so I said to the man, "Just watch." I then said in a louder and firmer voice, "Two!"

Briana was beginning to think about how she was going to have to get off soon or face the consequences.

I shouted, "Three!"

She immediately climbed down off the horse and ran to me, grabbing my hand to walk into the store.

I said to the man who was still watching, "It works for me!"

There is more than one toolbox in our home. My (Joey's) woodworking tools are all in my basement workshop in our house. There are toolboxes on shelves in our garage with tools I use in the garden and on the car.

One toolbox is stuck in the rafters of the garage. Do you want to know what is in it? By the end of this chapter, it will be full of tools we hope you put away, never to use again.

Counting 1-2-3

Not long after this shopping trip, we attended the parenting conference where we first heard about getting our kids to come to us when we called their names.

We asked about counting to three, indicating it worked for us. The conference speaker asked us why our kids came when we got to the count of three. I (Joey) did not hesitate in telling him they knew what they would get if they didn't. He asked me why we didn't give the consequence on the count of one, or to put it another way, when our children did not obey our instruction.

We realized we counted to three because both of our parents had done so with us. We decided then and there that we would expect obedience when we gave instructions. After all, our kids were going to one day get too old for us to count to three. What would we do then?

To give our children the consequence when they didn't obey immediately instead of after counting to three made a lot of sense to us. Remarkably, our kids made a quick adjustment to this change in our parenting.

Delayed Obedience

Either our children do what we ask them to do when we ask them to do it or they don't. Why do kids wait to follow through on an instruction you give them? Most likely it is because they don't want to do what you have instructed them to do.

If you have a child in fifth grade or above who doesn't do what you ask him to do because he is doing schoolwork or something similar, you can ask him when he thinks he can get to it.

If your child doesn't want to stop what nonessential thing he is doing, just doesn't want to do it, or is too lazy to do it, this is a different story. Do your kids have the right to choose when they will obey? Only you can answer this question as it applies to your children.

When kids don't get to the assigned task right away, for the most part they will choose to forget to get around to it at all. They are hoping you forget you gave it to them, which busy parents often do. The problem of children "forgetting" to get the job done is the number one reason for not allowing delayed obedience in your home.

Quiet children look for ways to disobey that won't get your attention. For example, they frequently delay their obedience. They fill their time with what they want to do or other tasks and say they didn't remember to complete the instruction when they are caught.

Children who delay following through with the instruction right away will need motivation (consequences) to remember to get instructions completed when they are given to them.

If your children do not obey until you yell at them or threaten them with consequences, this is another form of delayed obedience. They are not obeying if they don't complete the task until they know they have pushed you over the edge or they sense you are getting ready to push them over it.

You can resolve this. Don't threaten them with consequences. So what's wrong with threatening your children with consequences?

Stop Front-Loading Consequences

"Natalie!" yelled her mom. "If you do that again, you won't get to watch television for a month!"

Parents who threaten consequences rarely follow through with giving them because they were angry when they threatened to give them. Often, when they have calmed down, they don't remember what they said.

With young children, you can tell them in advance what the consequence will be if they do not comply. This is different than threatening them with a consequence.

"Ethan, when you won't say please when you want something, the answer will be no."

Parents who calmly tell a young child in advance what the consequence for not obeying will be tend to follow through with giving them. When your children reach elementary school age, you need to stop front-loading the consequence by telling them upfront what it will be.

"Dad!" cried Bradley. "You didn't tell me you were going to take away the computer if I didn't get my schoolwork done. Why didn't you tell me?"

Bradley will never submit (because he wants to) if he doesn't moves away from obeying because he has to. If you keep front-loading the consequences, your children will obey because of the fear of consequences. This will never lead to them doing what they are supposed to do from a heart of submission.

When your child doesn't obey, give him the consequence with no warning.

Misusing Grace

"Emma," called Mom. Her mom hears nothing but silence as she waits for a response. "Emma!" her mom called again. There still was no response, so her mom went looking for Emma and found her in her bedroom.

"Emma, what are you doing?" asked her mother. "I have been calling you, and you didn't respond."

"Oh, Mom," Emma replied, "I was so engrossed in my book that I didn't hear you."

"Okay," said her mom, "I will let it go this time, but I need you to come when I call your name next time."

"Okay," Emma replied, without looking up from her book.

About an hour later, her mother tried calling Emma again and got no response. She found Emma still reading in her room. Mom wanted to know why Emma didn't respond to her.

"Well," Emma told her, "I heard you, but I thought you would figure out I was still reading. This is a great book, and I am at the best part."

"I really need you to set the table for dinner," said her mother.

"Can I please finish this chapter? I am almost done."

"Okay." Her mom sighed. "Come down when you are finished."

Her mom was getting ready to call everyone to dinner when she saw the dishes weren't on the table. Emma ran downstairs when she heard her mom loudly call her name.

"I'm sorry, Mom. I meant to stop reading," Emma said. "I will do better next time."

"Okay, honey," Her mom replied. "Let's get it done together."

God our Father has given us the example we need to parent. He is merciful and He gives us grace. We should give our children the same.

"Grace" is defined as *"exemption from a penalty, a reprieve."*[1] This means you are getting something you have not earned and do not deserve. Too often, however, parents misuse grace. They do this by giving it too often and at inappropriate times, trying to win their children's love and approval, as the scenario above illustrated.

If parents are giving grace when their children deserve a consequence and then, out of frustration, give a consequence at some point in time for the same misbehavior, young children do not know what they did to deserve it.

When parents don't give consequences, they expect their children to monitor their own behavior, and until they reach the teen years (and perhaps not even then), children don't have the maturity or self-control to do so.

When children are out of control, they are begging their parents to bring them back under control, and it will take consequences to do this. Read any book in the Old Testament, and you will plainly see that God gave consequences to His children when they didn't obey Him. Why then do we think we can raise children who will love God with all their hearts without them?

When Giving Grace Is Appropriate

Your daughter made her bed every day for a week and then misses a day. Don't give her a consequence. Give her grace. If she makes her bed the next day and then doesn't do it the next two days, she needs a consequence to remind her that she needs to do it every day.

When you give your kids grace, you should tell them you are doing so and ask them what "grace" means. Otherwise, they know you saw their misbehavior and you chose not to do anything about it. They will think they got away with it.

If your child is overtired or sick or your family's schedule has been crazy, these would be appropriate times to give grace when your child doesn't obey. In other words, giving grace is absolutely appropriate when your children's behavior is not their fault, especially when it is yours. Why are they overtired? How did your family's schedule get so busy there is not a consistent bedtime? We all too often expect our kids to behave when it is not possible for them to do so.

Remember, grace is a gift. If you give too many gifts to your children, they will become spoiled and ungrateful. The same applies to the gift of grace. It is wise to have firm perimeters in mind regarding when you give it and why.

"For it is by grace you have been saved, through faith—and this not from yourselves; it is the gift of God, not by works so that no one can boast."
Ephesians 2:8-9

Allowing a Bad Attitude

When children do what they have been instructed to do with a bad attitude, all too often, the only consequence they get is a lecture or reminder from their parents to straighten up. What percentage of the time does your child straighten up? What do you do when he does? A word of encouragement or praise would be good. What do you do when he doesn't?

Often, parents don't do anything other than lecture their kids. Children do not have to straighten up when they know their parents will not do anything about their bad attitude. A wise man once told us that, in everything we do or don't do, we are teaching our children something. What are you teaching your children when you don't deal with their bad attitude?

Children need consequences for bad attitudes because having a good attitude is part of the obedience process. When children have a good attitude, they will give you the action, for their attitude, good or bad, drives their action.

Partial Obedience

In 1 Samuel 15, there is an interesting story that took place during the time Samuel was Israel's great prophet of God. The Amalekites (the bad guys) had opposed Israel when they left Egypt. God wanted them to know the consequences for messing around with His people. Through Samuel, He told King Saul to kill them all, including their livestock.

Saul won the battle. There was a problem with his victory, however. It did not please God. *"The word of the Lord came to Samuel: I regret that I have made Saul king, for he has turned back from following me and has not performed my commandments."* [2]

Saul won the battle. Why wasn't that good enough for God? What more did God want? God wanted Saul to obey His instructions to him all the way. Saul did not do what God told him to do. He did not kill the king of Amalek, nor the sheep and oxen. Worse than that, he set up a monument to himself in honor of his victory. His victory? He obviously forgot that he was just the tool God chose to use to accomplish what He wanted to do. The victory belonged to God and Him alone.

Samuel showed up, and Saul told him, "I have performed the commandments of the Lord!"

Isn't this like your children? They come to you and tell you they have done what you asked them to do when they only did part of the task. Samuel told Saul he could hear the sheep bleating. He got caught.

Amber, your nine-year-old daughter told you she was finished picking up her room. Yet the pillows were still on the floor next to her bed, and her clothes were thrown in a pile on the floor near her dresser. When you ask her about this, she tells you her room looks good enough for her, and she likes it this way.

Marcus, your thirteen-year-old son, told you he was getting his homework done. After he was in bed, you found it lying unfinished on the couch. Children are masters at partly obeying. They do the bare minimum, hoping to get by.

Saul actually came up with a pretty good excuse. He said the people (letting himself off the hook), wanted to sacrifice the animals to God. This should please God, right? Who decided to make the sacrifice? Saul did, once he was caught. Do your children come up with plausible excuses? Do they think you will let them off the hook when you find out the truth? Do you?

God noticed what Saul didn't do, and as a consequence, Saul was removed from being the king of Israel. That was a pretty stiff consequence for what could be considered not doing the little things. After all, they did win the battle (the big thing). Most Christians, at one time or another want to believe God will overlook the little things, as Saul did when he didn't kill the animals or the king.

God clearly shows us in this passage that He does not. He doesn't rate anything big or little; either you did obey or you didn't.

When God gives a command or instruction, the ones He gives it to do not have the right to negotiate it with Him or do it on their terms. God does not tolerate partial obedience from His children, and we should not tolerate it from ours. Partial obedience is not obeying completely. In reality, partial obedience is disobedience because, when it comes to obedience, either your child obeys all the way or he doesn't obey at all.

Put These Tools Away!

These are the tools you want to put away so you will stop using them. They are:

- Counting to Three

- Delayed Obedience

- Misusing Grace

- Allowing Bad Attitudes

- Partial Obedience

Well, as you can see, there is a reason this toolbox is stuck in the attic of the garage where no one can reach it. We will put more things in this toolbox later, but for now, you may see areas you need to work on in your parenting.

Our younger two sons, ten and twelve years at the time, had the responsibility to empty the clean dishes out of the dishwasher each day. They knew they were to make sure they inspected the dishes to ensure they were completely clean as well as put them in the cupboard. We had occasionally gotten a bowl out for breakfast in the morning to discover it was put away with a leftover residue of oatmeal or chocolate from the day before. After numerous attempts of trying to get our boys to pay closer attention, we decided to raise the stakes.

After discovering another bowl not completely clean, all the bowls and cups were pulled out of the cupboard, and we called the boys downstairs. We showed them the dirty bowl we had found and then pointed to all of the dishes on the counter. "Since we found this dirty bowl this morning, we are not sure the rest of these are clean, so you will wash them by hand, dry them, and put them back in the cupboard." Since that morning, we have not had any further issues with dirty dishes, the lesson about partial obedience hitting home.

We have been using the principles shared in this book since our oldest, now eighteen years old, was a toddler. I (Ken) travel almost full time during the week with my work, and I am so grateful we learned early on to train our children in obedience, as Karen serves as a single parent in my absence. I am not sure how she would have been able to do this with five active children if they did not obey. The teaching you are finding as you read is invaluable to parents. There have certainly been times when we have wondered if we would ever see the fruit of our efforts, but as your children grow and mature, the beauty you will find in their hearts and souls is priceless.

—Ken and Karen, Colorado

"Behold, to obey is better than sacrifice."
1 Samuel 15:22

CHAPTER 5

FIRST THINGS FIRST

Joanie came to the parenting class looking like she had just gotten out of bed. Her hair was not combed, and she wore sweats that looked like rags. You could tell she didn't want to be at the class. Her pediatrician had referred her to the class after the school counselor said she needed to get some help for her five-year-old son.

Joanie had not been to church since she was a kid, and fragments of stories she had heard there was all she knew about the Bible. Joanie believed in God but didn't understand why she needed a personal relationship with Jesus Christ. After a few weeks of listening and absorbing what she was hearing in class, God began to work in her life.

We talked with Joanie several times a week, helping her implement the principles and applications she was learning in class. She began fixing her hair better, wearing makeup, and dressing differently. In the way she walked and talked, you could see a new confidence in her whole being, and her parenting as well. Joanie was seeing real victories with her son and in her own life.

Toward the end of the class, Joanie started looking like she had when she first started, on the outside as well as the inside. You could tell her newfound confidence was badly shaken. Joanie told us she had chosen to correct her son for not coming to her when she called his name.

Her live-in boyfriend (who was not the boy's father) told her son, "Mommy doesn't love you because she doesn't let you have your own way. I love you and will always let you do what you want."

From that moment on, Joanie realized she knew the class and teaching worked, it just didn't work for her. We were disappointed for Joanie, but she had made her choice, a boyfriend over the training of her son. This taught us a huge lesson. Both parents must be on the same page to be successful in their parenting goals.

Just as it takes both a man and a woman to create a child, it also takes a mom and a dad to raise a child. Now, we understand some of you reading this are single parents. If your children are in second grade and older, we encourage you to find someone in your church of the opposite gender of yourself who would be willing to serve as a mentor-friend to your child.

A parent of one of your child's close friends who has the same values you are raising your child with is a good candidate. Or, as senior adults enjoy being asked to help, we encourage you to look for one whose family does not live in the area. When they don't have family close by, they have time to give to children they are not related to.

We also encourage you to make friends as a family with two-parent families. Children need to see healthy husband-and-wife relationships so they have models for their future marriages. Take the initiative and invite a family out for pizza with your family.

Getting Rid of the Baggage

Sharing common beliefs and values are important in a marriage, and when Carla and I came into our marriage, we knew we were like-minded in that regard. We were supportive of each other's goals and expectations. We didn't have any reason to believe this would change once we started having children.

How wrong we were! I entered parenting lugging a big, heavy bag full of "how I was raised" in each hand. Carla came into our parenting lugging her own bags that were heavier because her parents were divorced.

In my bags were the rules I had grown up with and how we were and were not going to raise our children. Carla's bags held the same. Only her rules were far different than mine were. We started butting heads in the delivery room as she prepared to give birth to our first child.

Like most men, I (Joey) felt Carla had a bit of a head start on parenting because of her babysitting experience and her love for children. Carla felt she had a huge head start on parenting because she was a woman, not because of her high school babysitting experience or college degree in social work. She was the mom, and that was all that mattered. I, of course, objected to this rationale. While changing diapers was not my thing (which was a temporary affliction), if Carla did something I didn't agree with, she was going to hear about it from me.

Now, most of the information in both of our bags was full of what we were not going to do with our kids. We are sure we are not alone on this. Being Christians, we were both firm that we were going to use the Bible as our guide to raise our children with. This was one thing we were both raised with that we were in complete agreement with.

At that time, it was often said the Bible didn't say a lot about parenting. The Bible does however, say all we need to know about how to live and we wanted to teach our children this from God's perspective. We did not have a plan on how we were going to accomplish this, and we both thought our way was best.

We wish we had known then the importance of being on the same page when it came to parenting. It would have saved us a lot of stress in our marriage and home. It is our hope and prayer that reading this book will give you and your spouse the opportunity to talk about your parenting and come into agreement on how to handle situations that come up with your kids.

So, for those of you who are married, try asking your spouse if you can read him (or her) a chapter once or twice a week before you go to bed. Explain to your spouse how important it is to get on the same parenting page.

If this doesn't work, try to find times that you can share key points you are learning with your spouse and how you want to change the way you handle your kids. Talk together about what you are learning. Getting on the same parenting page is one of the most valuable tools you have in raising your children.

Make Your Marriage a Priority

While getting on the same parenting page is an important tool for successful parenting, making your marriage a priority is equally important.[1] When children come into the family, they often become the most important people in the family, and the marriage relationship gets put on the back burner.

We had been married for almost four years when Michael joined our family. I (Carla) was overjoyed to be a mother, and I was more than ready to have this precious bundle in my arms. When Michael was around six months old, we drove to visit my father, who lived about ninety minutes away. We left Michael with his grandparents for the evening, and we were going out on a much-anticipated date for our wedding anniversary.

Joey took me to a nice hotel, telling me he needed to check out the rooms as a site for a potential youth conference. When we got to the room, he told me he was kidnapping me for the night. He had packed my clothes! I should have been delighted, but I was furious. How dare he think I wanted to be away from Michael all night?

We made the decision when we were first married that instead of giving each other gifts each year for our anniversary, we would go to a hotel and have a special date together, even if all we could afford was one night. Joey was determined this anniversary and all that followed were not going to be different.

He was right to show me that I needed to refocus my attention on our marriage relationship. We still have pictures of my dad sitting in a recliner holding Michael, who spent that night crying for his mommy. It was good for him to learn he could be with others as well.

Keeping a marriage healthy and loving over the years takes work, yet the rewards are immeasurable. We encourage you to try to find one way every day to show your spouse you love him/her.

Respecting Each Other's Differences

Kim was afraid she was messing up her kids or would squelch their emotions by being too hard on them.[2] She didn't want to give her kids consequences because she was afraid she would damage her children's emotions. Darren, her laid-back husband, was standing nearby quietly listening while his wife talked with us. I (Joey) knew he was hoping I would be able to talk some sense into her.

When asked why he had not stepped in to help her, Darren had a dumfounded look on his face. As the head of the home, his wife needed his help in parenting their children. Kim needed his encouragement that she was doing the right thing when dealing with the kids. She needed him to bring balance to their overall parenting. He didn't have a clue.

This couple wasn't seeing the strengths and weaknesses of each other; nor were they seeing how they needed to work together at parenting their four children, all under the age of six years.

Introducing them to the concept of temperaments opened their eyes. A person's temperament is the inborn, God-given part of his personality. [3] One's environment plus temperament makes up one's overall personality. There are four temperaments:

- A choleric is a born leader yet struggles with anger

- A sanguine is a happy-go-lucky individual but is impulsive and disorganized

- While a phlegmatic is the original couch potato, people call him in crisis because of his negotiating skills

- The perfectionistic melancholy is creative and organized, yet full of gloom and doom

While everyone have aspects of all four temperaments, it is common to have a blend of two, a primary and a secondary.

Km's primary temperament is melancholy, one that works off her emotions, which is why she had trouble setting them aside when dealing with her kids. She was fearful she would lose the love of her children when she corrected them.

On the other hand, her husband's primary temperament is phlegmatic, the one that hangs back and doesn't interfere unless he has to. When it comes to temperaments, opposites really do attract. This couple, like most of us, was drawn together because of the strengths of their temperaments and at first, was willing to accept the weaknesses.

Over time, the very things that first attracted them to each other became stumbling blocks to keep them from working together on the same page in their marriage and parenting.

Learning to Work Together

Carla was a wonderful stay-at-home mom, and I was very busy with ministry. I was ready for a break when I got home each day and only wanted to kiss my wife, catch up on sports on the television, and go play with the kids ... in that order.

One day, I called Michael before I left the church office, telling him we would play catch in the backyard when I got home. Carla quickly informed me that Michael did not have the freedom to play, meaning he was in trouble. I let her know Michael and I needed to have this time together. She told me one more time that Michael did not have the freedom to play anything with anyone.

Frustrated because she had been telling me this every day that week, I asked her when she was going to let him play ball with me. She suggested I ask him.

Not taking the hint, I continued to argue with her. She was angry with me because all I wanted to do when I got home was have fun with the kids. Since I did not get much time with them, this made perfect sense to me. This put her in the position of being the one who had to tell both the kids and her husband, "No."

Michael realized this, and he was an expert at playing us against one another. Michael would call me "Fun Daddy." When Carla heard one of our daughters refer to her as "Mean Mommy," things began to get rocky in our home.

We went camping on our vacation that summer, and Carla told me as we arrived at the campground that it was her turn to be the fun mommy and I was going to get to spend the week being the mean daddy. I smiled, thinking this was going to be no problem. This was my chance to show her how to do it right.

She was true to her word, and I spent the week chasing after the kids, yelling at them to do what I was telling them to do while she played with them whenever she wanted to, regardless of what I was trying to get them to do. Let's just say my admiration for my wife and disgust with myself for how I had been treating her greatly increased after that week.

Things changed when we got home. I would call Carla on my way home from church, and she would tell me what privileges each of the kids no longer had and gave me one thing she wanted me to work on with each child when I got home.

She knew as I tried to put the workday behind me, I would not remember more than one thing for each child. As I took over where she left off each day, the kids began to see consistency in the way we handled them, and their overall behavior improved.

In the midst of parenting, we learned to make our marriage special. We would go out on a date at least twice a month, if not weekly. I (Joey) planned our date nights, including getting the babysitter. One date a month, we called the "kids' date." We had an agenda on those dates to talk about the kids. We didn't allow any kid talk on the other dates we had that month.

On the kids' date, Carla brought me up to speed on the kids and showed me what she needed my help with and where I needed to step in when she was working with the kids. She also told me what they were doing well at, so I could praise and encourage them for these things.

We evaluated where each of the kids were at in regards to all four parts of obedience and what we needed to work on with each of them. It gave us the opportunity to work together when there was no conflict to deal with.

We decided what consequences would be appropriate for given offenses. Carla wrote them down and kept them in the kitchen where the kids couldn't see them, but we could. Having predetermined consequences gave us both the assurance we were doing the right thing.

Even though we talked about the kids every day, having this night designated to talk things through allowed us to rely on each other's strengths instead of fighting each other's weaknesses. This helped bring balance to our relationship.

I Don't Want to Fight Anymore

Getting on the same parenting page may cause intense discussions between a man and wife. Another word for "intense" would be discussions that turn negative. Yes, getting on the same parenting page can cause fights between spouses.

After all, when they say opposites attract, they don't tell you this means you won't think the same way as your spouse does, which will cause conflict because you can't agree on how to handle the kids. Lest we be accused of causing stress in marriages, here are some ways to fight fair with your spouse: [4]

- **Confront only when resolution is possible.** The one doing the confronting must be willing to change or compromise to meet the other spouse halfway. If not, what is the point of the confrontation? One spouse might be more willing to compromise when he or she sees the other is. The goal of confrontation should always be resolution.

- **Decide what the root problem is.** When two spouses cannot agree on how to raise their children, something is at the root of this problem. Does the husband expect his wife to do all the training of their children because he works long hours and often travels with his job?

Is the stay-at-home mom jealous that her husband gets to be with other adults at work? The root problem cannot be addressed until you both know what it is. The surface issues will never go away until the root problem is resolved.

- **Be prepared to offer solutions.** Most men are doers and fixers, meaning they want to do something to solve or fix the problem. It frustrates them when their wives throw some issue at them with no suggestions to resolve it, and husbands either get mad or won't talk. If you want to train your children to obedience as you learned in this book, start with sharing with your spouse how to do it "immediately." Ask him or her to do one new thing, like calling the kids' names and wait to hear a "Yes, Mom/Dad" before giving the instruction. When they see success with this, ask your spouse to do one more new thing.

- **Take a good look at yourself first.** Take an objective look at your own shortcomings and where you might be at fault in this situation. You say your spouse is never open to new ideas. If we were to talk to him or her, we might be told that you are not consistent with following through with new ideas you come up with, so why bother?

Or your spouse might tell us that you will complain about the way he or she does everything you suggest and your spouse knows he or she will never do it well enough to please you, so why try? So, look at yourself first, for the only person you can truly change is yourself.

- **Argue the problem, not the person.** When a confrontation arises between spouses, resolution is quicker and easier when the confronting spouse sticks to attacking the problem, not his or her spouse. How can you do this? Stick to the facts. Otherwise, you will get off on tangents and won't maintain perspective.

Don't use statements that start with, "You always…" or "You never…" Your spouse will immediately start defending himself/herself and will come up with a time he or she did or did not. Don't place blame or make excuses.

- **Allow your spouse to express his or her feelings.** If you want your spouse to listen to you, then you need to be prepared to listen to him/her first. Real listening means you are not preparing the next thing you will say while your spouse is talking. It also means that you are not constantly interrupting your spouse while he or she is talking. Be quiet and listen!

- **It is not what you say; it is how you say it.** You can say the exact same thing you were fighting about in a different tone of voice, and it will carry a completely different meaning. If you start to raise your voice, end the discussion, and set a time to finish it later.

- **Be willing to forgive.** If your spouse does not come around to seeing things the way you want him/her to, realize this is not the time to discuss it and move on. Do what you can both agree on.

> *"Be completely humble and gentle,*
> *bearing with each other in love."*
> *Ephesians 4:2*

Getting on the Same Parenting Page

To get on the same parenting page, we would like to encourage you both to take a look at what is in the baggage you each brought to the marriage. Is your spouse fond of saying, "We will not parent the way your mother did?" If so, find out exactly what your mother did that is so offensive to your spouse. Instead of getting angry, talk about what you can do instead of what your mother did that your spouse does not agree with.

At the same time, talk about the things you each think your parents did right. This talk needs to take place when you are both open-minded and willing to hear what the other has to say.

We recommend you and your spouse agree on what obedience is and how to get it. Decide together what your methods of correction will be and how you will use them, how much is too much, and what is appropriate.

This will mean you have to communicate as to what you think is right and why. We all have opinions and feelings as to what is right and what is wrong. Does the Scripture support them? The two of you need to agree what is right and wrong from God's Word and how He wants you to raise the children He has given you.

Children Will Have Baggage Too

Your children will carry baggage into their marriages someday. Whether married or single, work to put into your children's baggage what they and their future spouses will want to parent their children with.

When we were introduced to this material, one of the most life-changing teachings for my husband and I was the importance of the husband and wife relationship. This seems so basic, and we knew it was necessary and commanded by God, but we didn't realize how vital it was to our parenting.

I used to get mad when my husband would discipline the kids because, being a permissive parent, I thought he was too harsh. The kids knew I was on their side, so they didn't listen to their dad. I justified my attitude by thinking I knew the kids better than he did. After all, I am the one who spends all day with them and has a better understanding of the context of the situation, which I seldom communicated with my husband. There was a lot of tension in our marriage because of this.

Through the teaching shared in this chapter, I realized we are both on the same team and are working toward the same goal, which could only be achieved if we work together. I now welcome my husband's contributions to our parenting. I love having a partner that I can call on anytime to talk over a discipline issue with and know I have his support before I take action. Learning to put our marriage relationship first has brought us closer together, and we now stand as a team in raising our children.

—Tom and Cherie, Iowa

"Submit to one another out of reverence for Christ."
Ephesians 5:21

CHAPTER 6

KEEP PLUGGING AWAY

O ur son attended the middle school across the street from our home. He was doing well in school, getting very good grades. He was well-liked by his teachers and friends. Hearing this, you might be surprised to find out we consider these years to have been our biggest challenge in parenting Michael.

We had been struggling with him for a long time. We worked on getting obedience and thought we had it with him. For the most part, he came when we called him with a decent attitude. Yet we were dealing with other things that had gotten out of hand, and it wasn't pleasant, as Michael never yielded quickly or quietly.

We knew we were missing something but could not figure out what it was. There were little things he wasn't hitting the mark on, and they were beginning to add up. One day when I (Joey) called his name, Carla noticed he didn't say "Yes, Dad." He simply said, "Yes."

Carla started listening when she called him and realized he was just saying "Yes" to her too. We talked to him about it, and he just smiled. He knew exactly what he was doing.

Michael had changed the rules of the game, and he was waiting to see when we would notice. Some might not think this is a big deal. It was a big deal to Michael because he was taking control.

Michael was on a three-week cycle. He would find a way to slide around coming to us the way he had been instructed to, and after many reminders and lectures, he would receive consequences. He would then bring his level of obedience back up to speed and keep it at the standard we required for about three weeks, when the cycle started all over again. Who was in control here, us or Michael?

If you asked us this question a few weeks earlier, we would have told you we were. Once we realized Michael was deciding when and how he was going to obey, we knew he was in control. It was time to get back to the basics of training him to all four parts obedience.

Carla looked at me and asked, "Why do we have to get back to it? Why don't we just keep him there?"

While this is not revolutionary thinking, it did start a revolution in our home. We decided to hold each other accountable and pay closer attention to how he responded to us.

Michael kicked it in gear in the other areas we were dealing with due to some painful consequences, so things were running smoothly. Sure enough, about three weeks later, Carla noticed that instead of saying "Yes, Mom" when she called his name, he came immediately to her and nodded his head.

She waited a bit, called him again, and got the same response. She gave him a consequence, and other things didn't get out of control as a result of catching this when it first happened.

It's a Monkey Wrench

A lack of *consistency* is the biggest monkey wrench in parenting. Like many of you, we waited until something blew up in our faces until we took it on. Children rarely cross a line or push a boundary to the point their parents are pulling out their hair on impulse. They nudge that boundary for quite some time until it gets so far off track parents finally take notice.

When parents are inconsistent in the way they manage the boundaries they put in their children's lives, they are giving their children gaps for them to slide through. As a result, kids take too many freedoms.

What do we mean by "freedoms?" Some freedoms are earned, meaning kids have earned the right to not have to ask permission to do something. As kids mature and grow, they should be earning age-appropriate freedoms.

Kids also take freedoms they haven't earned. They do this when they do things they are not supposed to do or don't have permission to do. We yell at our kids when, in reality, we should be yelling at ourselves.

There are four primary reasons why parents struggle with being consistent when parenting:

- Parents are too busy

- Their busyness makes them too tired

- Parents don't know what to do

- Parents are working on too many things at one time

Are You Too Busy and Too Tired?

Parents are too busy to be focused on parenting, and the busyness of their lives makes them too tired to pay attention to the seemingly little things going on with their children.

Parents are busy spending time with extended family members, volunteering for church events, working long hours, participating in exercise programs or social networking, going to their kids' activities or engaging in entertainment, hobbies, and projects at home and in the yard, just to name a few.

Focus on the Inward, Not the Outward

So, how do you become un-busy? We recommend you start with your kids' activities. Even though all the events (sports, music, art) they could participate in are good in and of themselves, a child does not need to participate in all of them. Keeping children busy is a way of keeping them entertained, but over the long haul, it wears kids out.

Our daughter Amy had a piano student who never had time to practice. She was talented and could have become proficient on the piano and keyboard. Amy structured this child's lesson so twenty minutes of practice a day would be sufficient for the student to progress. Amy suggested she practice ten minutes in the morning before school and ten minutes in the evening.

The student's mother told Amy her daughter couldn't practice for that amount of time each day because she had an activity she had to go to every day after school. This young lady was exhausted and often told Amy she wanted to play the piano but was too busy and too tired to practice.

Amy dropped her as a student and asked her mother not to find another teacher. Amy told this mom she was throwing away the money she spent on lessons because her daughter was not progressing in her ability to play the piano.

Were all these activities good? Yes. Were they all good for this child? Definitely not. Nor were they good for the child's mother, who spent every afternoon hauling her kids to and from one activity after another.

During our children's high school years, they all participated in band. At band competitions or concerts, rarely were all the band students present. Many were in sports events that were scheduled for the same time. Sports came first at the school, and the students were instructed to participate in those events over band. We felt sorry for the band director as he rarely knew who he could count on for music events.

When parents plan too many activities for their kids to participate in or allow their teens to get involved in too many themselves, they have fallen into the trap of emphasizing outward abilities over inward character.

Rather than schedule another activity for your children to participate in, consider scheduling time to train your children in character values that reflect the heart of Christ. Character determines the way a person acts, and it is up to parents to send their kids into adulthood with character that will direct them to successful, godly living.[1] No one will do it for you.

Once you get your kid's activities under control, it is time to look at your schedule. Our daughter Briana was pulled out of public school in fourth grade for medical reasons. The teacher the school assigned to oversee her education dropped off her schoolwork on Monday and picked it up on Friday. I (Carla) started homeschooling on the spot. As a result, things weren't getting done at home in a timely manner. I stopped going to a women's Bible study, learned to use the slow cooker to get dinners on the table on time, and lowered my expectations about how clean the house needed to be.

How can you whittle down your activities and expectations? Look for ways to slow down your life. It used to be unheard of for a family not to sit down and eat their supper together. Nowadays, it can be a rare occurrence. Please don't let this happen to your family.

It is not a sin to choose not to participate in every activity or event. When you slow down your schedule, your bodies will slow down too, and you will not be so tired.

Get Sleep

Tired kids and tired parents do not make a happy family. On any given day, the behavior of an overly tired person, child or adult, can be off-kilter, causing tension in the family.

Studies show forty-seven million adults say they do not get enough sleep to be alert the next day. Millions of people miss work every day because of health problems caused by lack of sleep. Seventy million people say they drive when they are drowsy. In over one hundred thousand police-reported car accidents last year, drivers fell asleep at the wheel, causing fifteen hundred deaths and seventy-one thousand permanent injuries to unfortunate people.[2]

In our culture today, there is an epidemic of exhausted kids and adults because our lives have become too busy. Is it worth it?

Do You Know What to Do?

Parents are also inconsistent with training their children because they don't know what to do when their children do not stay within the boundaries they have set for them. They don't know what consequences to give, so they lecture, remind, and yell instead.[3]

We had been doing this with Michael. At the time of the opening scenario, he was twelve years old. What good were lectures and reminders? He knew what he was supposed to do. How would a lecture or reminder get him to do the right thing? Michael waited until we were done talking. He nodded his head and went on his way.

Consequences are the reminders that kids need to choose to do what is right. Sit down with your spouse, list two behaviors for each of your children that have become problematic, decide on a consequence to use when they misbehave in these areas, and stick to it. When parents are consistent in giving the same painful consequence for a given misbehavior, they will see their children step up their level of compliance. When children start to pull up their compliance in the areas their parents are working with them on, a domino effect often occurs, and you will see them pull it up in other areas as well

Pulling Weeds

So, can you be consistent? Yes, you can. It will take work. What is more important in your life right now than raising your kids to shine for the glory of God? Disobedient children will grow into disobedient adults. How can God use people who will not obey?

Jodi, a mother of four children, shared this story with me (Carla) on the subject of being consistent in training her children to obedience. While taking her boys to the library for story time, Jodi walked past a woman working in the library's flower garden.

It was a scorcher that day, and she felt sorry for this poor woman with sweat dripping from her brow as she pulled at each weed stuck in the hard, dry ground. Jodi looked behind her and saw what seemed to be an endless strip of weeds that were just as tall as the flowers. Jodi knew she would be discouraged if she faced such a task.

A week later, Jodi and her kids went back to the library and noticed the lady had finished her job as they appreciated the now well-manicured flower garden. However, after all that hard work, Jodi already saw a few weeds popping up. Jodi thought of all the labor-intensive hours the lady could save herself if she had the foresight and determination to spend just a few minutes a day plucking up those pesky weeds.

Jodi realized this applies to parenting as well. God has given us a beautiful garden in our children, who are made in His image. God has given parents the job of being their child's gardeners. It is the parents' job to protect the garden's beauty and to weed the garden and prune the flowers to make it even more beautiful.

As life gets busy and parents are being pulled in many different directions, the weeds of disobedience quickly pop up one by one and soon take over the garden of their children's hearts. All you can see now are weeds and the work it will take to pull them out can be overwhelming.

Climb the Mountain One Step at a Time

When you look at your child's garden (heart), do you see more flowers or weeds? How diligent have you been as his gardener? Just like the woman in this story, keep your eyes focused on the one weed you need to be pulling. Don't look at all the other weeds that haven't been pulled yet. It is hard to stay focused on working on one thing at a time if you do.

The weed you are trying to pull should be getting your child to a higher standard in all four parts of obedience. Don't get distracted by the other weeds, no matter how tall they are. If you stay focused on the disobedient weed, you will eventually start to see progress.

Even though it gets hard and you are tired, don't give up! When you pull up weeds after a nice rainfall, the weeds come up with little effort. Maintenance is so much easier than digging weeds out of an overgrown garden. Over time, you will win the battle as you consistently work to pull each weed, and you will be able to see the beauty God intended to shine forth from your child. Pray daily for consistency, and keep yourself accountable to your spouse or someone else to help keep you from the three-week slide we went through with our son.

Throw Inconsistency Away

Are you too tired to deal with your child's disobedience? Remind yourself that you don't get a second chance at parenting and get moving. Are you too busy? Ask yourself if the things keeping you busy are more important from an eternal perspective than training your children in Godly character.

Are you talking to deaf ears? Give your kids the consequences they are begging you for. Do you need to work on de-scheduling your lives? If so, get to it. Throw the tool of inconsistency in that toolbox in the rafters of the garage.

Character Matters

We know you are committed to taking care of your children. But are you prepared for the time it takes to train them? Once your children consistently obey you, you can teach them the values God has put in place for daily living. What are these values? Galatians 5:22–23 shares many with us.

"The fruit of the Spirit is love, joy, peace, patience, kindness,
goodness, faithfulness,
gentleness and self-control."

Frankly, it can take all of the eighteen years your child is growing up for you to build these fruits into his heart. God wants us to teach children to not only be a valuable member of society, but to also have value in their character, spiritual growth, and moral development.

One's character is composed of thoughts and actions that become a permanent part of who you are. People will notice character that reflects the values of Christ, as these are uncommon traits in the world today.

When others notice the character of your children, they will see shining lights that will reflect the glory of God. Don't let inconsistency undermine the teaching and training you already have and still want to put into your children.

Does God want you to be legalistic, overbearing parents who demand obedience from your children? No, He doesn't, and it is our prayer this is not what you have gleaned from this book. He wants you to be loving, caring, understanding, and compassionate, yet at the same time, God expects us to have the strength to hold to His standards.

The process of training your children to obedience is not always a pretty or fun one, but once you get there, maintaining it is not difficult.

Lean on Me

Proverbs 3:5–6 says,

> *"Trust in the Lord with all your heart*
> *and lean not on your own understanding;*
> *in all your ways acknowledge Him,*
> *and He will make your paths straight."*

Oh, how much easier it is to trust in ourselves than in God. Whether new or experienced parents, we all tend to rely on our own instincts, do our own thing, and hope for the best. But this verse tells us in no uncertain terms that we are to rely on God's understanding.

Because God knows everything, relying on Him should not be difficult. Yet it is. Busyness is again a culprit. When our time is spent running from one event or activity to another, we don't have time to lean on God. Instead we lean on ourselves. This is what the book, *Wisdom for Parents* says about this verse:

> *The wise parent must develop his understanding of parenting but never lean on his own understanding. To fail to develop our understanding in this age of technology and mass communication is sin, but to lean on that knowledge is a greater sin. The more we add to our knowledge and the more we develop our skills, the more God will use them as He sees fit.*
>
> *But the danger is we will lean on them rather than trust God. How do we know we are leaning on God and not our own instincts and experience? By the time we spend in prayer! Trust in God and distrust in self can be measured in direct proportion to the amount of time you find yourself asking God for help and guidance in prayer.* [4]

Don't wait until you are in a desperate struggle to figure out what to do in your parenting before you turn to God in prayer. Be specific and ask Him to direct you to where you need to go to find the answers you are looking for.

There is never a time in our lives that God has not already surrounded us with all the resources we need to resolve an ongoing situation or circumstance we are dealing with. You cannot be consistent in your parenting unless you are consistent in leaning on Him. Leaning on yourself or other people apart from God will only lead to failure and defeat. Lean on Jesus for all the understanding you need in your parenting. He will never let you down.

Theory is good, but the teaching you are reading in this book is excellent in assisting in the practical application of parenting strategies. It helped us in getting to the heart of our children at an early age. We now have three teenagers and are enjoying the fruit of our efforts. Whether you are new to parenting or find yourself at a loss with your teens, the experience and expertise you are reading here will enable you to make headway that you thought was impossible to attain.

Joey and Carla helped us realize the importance of dealing with the inner attitude, not just the outward actions, and they taught us the importance of asking questions to draw out an understanding of where our children were in their thinking. All of that would have accounted for nothing if we had not learned to be consistent in our training efforts. We are so thankful to have learned the things they have shared here with you. We are often told what a joy our teens are to be around, and we know it is because we learned early on what obedience means and the importance of training your children to it.

—Stacy and Anne, Montana

"Let us not become weary in doing good,
for at the proper time we will reap a harvest
if we do not give up."
Galatians 6:9

CHAPTER 7

Do Compliant Kids Exist?

"Kids, your snack is ready. Come eat at the table." Carol set the plate of sliced apples covered with peanut butter on the table with cups of water for her children, seven-year-old Evan and five-year-old Tessa.

Evan, always in a hurry, was scooting around in his chair and dropped a slice of apple on the floor. When Evan tried to pick it up, he stepped on it, smearing peanut butter everywhere. When he climbed back into his chair, he knocked over his cup, spilling water all over the table. His frustrated mom told him to sit still and finish his snack while she cleaned up the mess.

Meanwhile, Tessa had wrapped her apple slices in a napkin and took them into the family room to eat while she was watching television. Carol was so busy dealing with Evan that she didn't notice as Tessa quietly slipped away. When Carol saw her in the other room, she praised Tessa for not making a mess while eating her snack.

What was Tessa's instruction? Was it to eat her snack at the table, or could she eat it anywhere as long as she didn't make a mess? Because it was to eat her snack at the table, she was inadvertently praised for her disobedience.

***

Bryan and Julia, excited to get some quality time together, were going out on a date. Before they left, they told fifteen-year-old Lily and twelve-year-old Andy to be in bed by teno'clock. Bryan and Julia had a great evening out, but they were surprised to find the kids up when they got home around eleven o'clock.

Lily was playing the piano, and Andy was watching television in a different room. Lily told them she had reminded Andy when it was time to go to bed, but he refused to go. When his parents confronted him, Andy angrily told them ten o'clock was too early for him to go to bed on the weekend and let them know how unfair they were. Andy was sent upstairs to his bedroom, followed by his parents who dealt with him there.

Meanwhile, Lily continued to play the piano. When her parents came downstairs after dealing with Andy, she told them she was going to play the song she was scheduled to perform at her piano recital that would take place in a few weeks one more time and then she would go to bed. Her parents told her they knew she would play well at the recital because she practiced so much and went to prepare for bed themselves.

When was Lily told to go to bed before her parents left on their date? Was it different from Andy's time? Why didn't she get in trouble like he did?

Many parents, if asked, would say they have an easy child and a defiant and angry child who never does what he is told to do. Because "easy" is defined here as doing what you are told to do, neither of the moms in the above scenarios have an easy child.

They each have a child who openly rebels by being defiant and throwing fits, either verbally or physically, and one who quietly rebels—pouting, sulking, whining, and "forgetting" to follow through with instructions. None of the children did what they were told to do. Tessa should have eaten her snack at the table, and Lily should have gone to bed at ten o'clock, whether her brother did or not.

When kids rebel, they resist the one in authority. Why would parents consider Evan and Andy's refusal to do what they were told to do rebellion and let the girls off the hook? We think it is because these two forms of rebellion look different to parents so they relate to them differently.

Does it look different to God? No, it doesn't because God looks at the heart, and what He saw in the hearts of Evan, Tessa, Andy, and Lily were children kicking and screaming because they did not want to do what they had been told to do.

While children who openly rebel are exhausting to work with, they are much easier to train than the child who rebels quietly. You might think we are out of our minds. We are not. Children who quietly or passively rebel are hard to catch because you often don't hear them or see them when they misbehave.

What did Tessa's mom teach her about snacks? She taught her as long as she did not make a mess, she could eat wherever she wanted to. What did Lily's parents teach her? She learned that as long as she was doing something good and didn't talk back to her parents, she didn't have to obey.

Are Tessa's parents going to figure out she is doing exactly what they have allowed her to do her entire life when she gets in trouble as a teen for going behind people's backs to get her own way? Lily's parents don't understand how she is getting "incompletes" in two of her classes for not finishing her papers. The teachers all love her because she helps them clean their classrooms and such, but they tell Lily's folks at a parent-teacher conference if she doesn't get her term paper turned in, she won't pass their class. Who will tell Lily it is wonderful that she is nice and helpful, but just because her teachers like her doesn't mean they will pass her? What children learn at a young age is displayed throughout their lives.

Is it Gender or Temperament?

We have heard it said, "Boys will be boys." Boys are different from girls in many ways. Boys are more physically active, especially during puberty. For the most part, they communicate through actions rather than words. They like to be outdoors and think balls, rocks, sticks, and things that squiggle are the best.

Girls, on the other hand, like to talk. They giggle and whisper and giggle some more. For the most part, girls like beautiful things. While these are certainly generalities, they are descriptive of the genders.

When you hear the statement, "Boys will be boys," however, it is usually said as punctuation for bad behavior. We are of the opinion temperaments have more to do with predicting behavior than gender does. It is easier for parents to focus on the weaknesses of their child's temperament because they deal with them every day.[1]

Kids with the choleric temperament, male or female, will get in your face, demanding to get their own way and will always find ways to take control. They are defiant, angry children and are difficult, but not impossible, to train. These kids are also born leaders and can see what needs to be done in a given situation and come up with a plan to get it done. They are definitely not quiet in their rebellion.

Children with the melancholy temperament won't try to do things they don't think they can be perfect at. They are moody, and if you don't meet their expectations, they are not afraid to confront you. They are also creative, artistic and musical, and are very good at whatever they put their minds to. They are a mixture of both forms of rebellion because, while they will pout, whine, and sulk, they are not afraid to tell you what they think either.

While they are the most talkative children you have, kids with the sanguine temperament are passive in their rebellion. They are delightful to be around because of their sunny dispositions, yet they are easily distracted and can't seem to remember what they have been told to do. We say they are quiet or passive in their rebellion, for it takes the form of "I forgot," "I don't remember," and so forth. These children will not verbally confront someone unless they have no choice in the matter.

Phlegmatic children quietly rebel in a different way. They are not talkers. If you tell a child with this temperament to stay in his room, when your back is turned, he will put his toes outside his bedroom door and smile. On the other hand, because they are peacemakers, they are good negotiators. They are incredibly stubborn, digging their heels in when they decide not to comply with an instruction given. They are the hardest to catch when they rebel because, unlike children with the choleric temperament, they don't need anyone to see their rebellion for it to be victorious to them.

When it comes to training quietly rebellious children, it is helpful to have insight into these temperaments and know what your children's temperaments are.[2]

Do You Need Binoculars?

How do you know if your child is quietly (or passively) rebelling? The definition of "passive rebellion" is *"resistance without resorting to violence or active opposition; not doing something required.*"[3] Quiet or passive rebellion takes the following forms:

- Does your child tell you he will do something he has been asked to do, but just doesn't seem to get around to it?

- Does your child sulk and pout when he doesn't get his own way?

- When you ask your child why something wasn't done he agreed to do, does he respond by saying, "I did this (something else) instead"?

- How often does your child say, "I forgot" or "I don't remember"?

- Does your child respond to questions you ask with "maybe," "perhaps," or "I'm not sure," or does he shrug his shoulders or roll his eyes?

- Does your child do part of the assigned task but never get around to completing it?

Your Child Can Remember!

Do you honestly believe when your child says, "Oh, I forgot" that he really did forget? We are letting you know your child did not forget. He chose not to remember.

If you think about it, is he capable of remembering to do something he wants to do or you have promised him he can do, no matter how far into the future it will take place? If you aren't sure what the answer is, test your children. Tell them you will take them for an evening of fun and pizza next Friday night. Don't say anything else about this all week.

See if they remember and remind you. We are guessing they will remember because it is something your children want to do.

So, your child is perfectly capable of choosing to remember what he wants to do and forgetting what he doesn't want to do. Children with the phlegmatic and sanguine temperaments don't want the responsibility "remembering" entails. It is easy for children to forget to do something rather than make themselves do something they didn't want to do in the first place.

Working With A Child Who is Not Remembering

The following are suggestions to work with a child (seven years of age and up) who is not remembering to get things done.

First, your children are counting on you to remind them when they forget to do something. As long as you keep reminding them, they never have to remember on their own.

Michael had friends who were brothers; one was in middle school and the other in fifth grade. The older boy was always ready for school on time, but the younger one rarely was. Their mom was always pushing him so they could get to the bus stop on time. Their mom finally decided she'd had enough, and she told her son on the following Monday he was getting no more reminders from her.

This young man didn't take his mom seriously, and on Monday, he was not ready for school on time. The mom sent her older son off to the bus stop. When her younger son missed the bus, he was astounded his mother had no intention of driving him to school as she had done many times before.

This time, his mother was armed with the knowledge that she had done everything possible to convince her son to be ready on time, and now consequences were going to have to motivate him to make the bus. After walking the mile to school that morning lugging a heavy band instrument, this boy managed to get to the bus on time the rest of the year.

When your child chooses to forget what you told him to do, have him sit in a chair until he remembers. Your child may cry, whine, pout, plead, and beg you to tell him once again what his instruction was. Resist the temptation to give in, unless you are really in doubt as to whether he did forget. If he concentrates hard enough, he will remember.

Initially, you may have to prompt him like this: "When you came home from school, you asked me if you could watch television, and I told you that you could as soon as you did what?" (The "what" never got done, which is why this conversation is taking place) Try not to accept generic answers such as "I forgot" or "maybe."

When your child remembers, and he will when he realizes you aren't going to tell him again and he doesn't have the freedom to get off the chair until he does, he should receive the consequence of losing the freedom of whatever he was doing instead.

When does he get the privilege again? He gets it back when you see him remembering to do his assigned tasks for a period of time. If you are consistent with this, you will be amazed at what your quietly rebellious child will start remembering to do.

When our Amy was around six years of age, she couldn't seem to remember what she was told to do. We would give her an instruction, and she would smile, nod her head, and tell us she would be glad to do it, yet the tasks rarely got done. When we asked her about it, she said she forgot to do them.

For a long time, we convinced ourselves that it was normal to forget to do things, so we reminded her what the instruction was.

One day, I (Carla) had lost all patience with Amy's forgetfulness. I gave her an instruction, and I could literally see it go in one ear and out the other. I waited a few minutes then asked her what she was supposed to be doing. It was no surprise she couldn't remember.

This was the first time I had her sit in a chair until she did remember. She begged me to tell her one more time what I had asked her to do. She told me she couldn't remember because I had not given her any reminders. She asked her sister when she walked by if she had heard what I told her to do.

It was a pitiful sight watching Amy try to remember, but I was determined we were going to find a way to lick this problem. After ten minutes or so, I told her I was going to tell her one more time what she was supposed to be doing, but this was the last time she would get a reminder from me. I stuck to my guns, and Amy started to choose to remember what she was told to do.

A couple years later, we decided to work with Amy on another trait of quietly rebellious children. When we asked Amy if she had made her bed as she came down for breakfast, she would answer, "maybe," "perhaps," "I think so," or her favorite, "I'll go check."

We started to say, "I asked you a question that requires either a yes or no answer. Which is it?"

She would respond by telling us the truth. She didn't do the assigned task.

"But above all…let your 'yes' be yes
and your 'no' be no…"
James 5:12

When children do things that are helpful instead of what they were told to do, the praise of grateful parents often rewards them. Resist praising your child for doing a different task if he didn't get the assigned task done first.

As I (Carla) mentioned earlier, I abruptly started homeschooling the girls due to Briana's medical issues when Briana was in fourth grade and Amy was in second grade. I couldn't figure out why Amy was having trouble getting her schoolwork completed on time. I complained to Joey at one point that, despite all my efforts in dealing with her, Amy was still not completing her schoolwork on time.

He looked at me and said, "What is she doing instead?"

Amy was finding all kinds of ways to be helpful around the house during school time, which she was, not insignificantly, receiving many words of encouragement for. We needed to take this on.

It was snowing outside. The girls were in the kitchen, and I could tell they were bickering, albeit quietly. I asked them what was going on.

Amy said, "Briana doesn't want to go out and help me shovel snow."

I started to get on Briana until Joey intervened. "Amy, what are you supposed to be doing right now?"

She said, "I don't know."

He told her, "Go get your school assignment sheet, and bring it to me."

She was supposed to be doing English.

He asked her if it was already completed. He had already guessed it was not. He then asked, "Did I instruct you to shovel the walks?" She admitted he had not.

He asked her, "Did your mother instruct you to shovel the walks?"

She looked at me and shook her head no.

Notice that his questions were deliberately worded in a way that required an answer of yes or no. After apologizing to her sister for misleading her, she was told to get back to doing her English, and Joey went out to shovel the walks, as he had intended to do all along.

The next morning, I went grocery shopping on my way home from the gym. Amy eagerly started putting away groceries as I brought them into the house. I started to tell her where I wanted an item to be put but caught myself in time.

I asked her, "What are you supposed to be doing right now?"

She was supposed to be doing science. I asked her if it was done.

She said, "It isn't, but I'll do it later."

I asked her if she would remember to get to it later.

She said, "I don't know."

Does this sound like a girl who intends to choose to remember to do her science?

She put her hands on her hips and said, "Most parents would be glad to have a child like me. Most parents would be grateful for my help!"

She was indignant, and she had to spend time in her room to find her happy attitude. I sighed deeply, knowing she was right. Most parents would be grateful for her helping hands. But her parents understood her refusal to do what she was supposed to do when she was supposed to do it was rooted in a heart that believed she didn't have to do what she didn't want to do.[4]

Taking Back the Reins

Observe your quietly rebellious child for a few days. Keep track of how often this child does what you have asked him to do. Don't remind him or repeat your instruction. Just watch and see. You might find your quietly rebellious child has taken the reins of control from you in areas you weren't even aware of.

The easiest way to get back in control is to step up your child's level of obedience. Sit down with your kids, and let them know you are disappointed in their level of obedience. After sharing with them once again how you want them to obey, let them know you will be watching.

The next morning, starting with your quietly rebellious child, call his name, and see what response you get. If it is not the response your children have been instructed to give, a warning is appropriate. The next time you call his name, if you don't get the correct response, a consequence is needed.

One More Time

- Children who are characterized by rebelling quietly are polite, well-mannered, respectful children.

- Be willing to correct these children consistently, even if you think their action or behavior is no big deal. What does not appear to you to be a big deal is a huge deal to quietly rebellious children.

- Deal with pouting, sulky, and nonverbal behaviors and attitudes as you would a full-blown temper tantrum.

- This child needs to apologize when confronted with his quietly rebellious behaviors.

- Keep tight boundaries to define where your quietly rebellious child is making choices and taking freedoms he hasn't earned.

- Force him to remember and give you straight answers to your questions.

Rooting Out Sins

It can take a long time to root out deep weeds of rebellious sin patterns. When rooting out sins of the heart, it takes time, effort, patience, and perseverance on the part of the parents.

If you are a single parent, we encourage you to enlist the help, encouragement, and assistance of your parents or a good friend or mentor to help you with the weeding process, as it can be mentally exhausting and physically draining.

If you are married, be encouraging of each other as you work on this together. We know from experience that it is easy to point out each other's faults, but this only causes more problems in the marriage and family.

Don't rush training your kids, thinking you have to have them completely trained now. Take the time to do it right. Do not be discouraged if you feel you have not been appropriately dealing with your quietly rebellious child.

We knew for a long time that there were root issues with Amy we were not on top of, but guiding her sister through the middle years with issues of her own was taking the majority of our time.

I remember saying to Amy, "I know there are issues with you that we are not catching at this time. I just want you to know if you do not start working on some of these things on your own, your day will come."

And it did.

Our oldest son, who is now eleven years old, is a compliant child by nature, but when his sister was born, we saw lots of his behaviors were not pretty. He was so good-natured that we had been allowing him to do his own thing. We really wanted him to obey and thought we knew how to get him there, but we didn't. We found we were asking him too many questions and negotiating with him rather than giving him a command to be followed.

We were blessed to be introduced to this practical information on obedience training, as it literally changed the tone of our home. We began calling our son by name and expecting him to respond. While it got worse before it got better, we persevered and were able to get him and his sister to a high level of obedience. We were able to see great benefits of having children who obeyed even when they didn't want to. Having obedient children has allowed us to work with them on additional and deeper character issues that we would not have been able to deal with had we not first obtained obedience from them.

Training children in obedience is hard because it takes a lot of effort on everyone's part, but it is worth it. It is up to us as Mom and Dad to continue to hold them accountable for what we have instilled in them. Striving to train our children in obedience has allowed us to have a clear direction in our parenting. Training our children to obedience helped build an incredible level of trust between our children and us. We have recently adopted twin three-year-old girls from another country. Training them in obedience using sign language (since they do not yet speak English) is going well. We have seen the beauty of obedience, and what a testament to the Lord obedient children are.

—Jason and Heather, Iowa

"What do you think? There was
a man who had two sons.
He went to the first and said,
'Son, go and work today in the vineyard.'
'I will not,' he answered, but later
changed his mind and went.
Then the father went to the other
son and said the same thing.
He answered, 'I will, sir,' but he did not go.
Which of the two did what his father wanted?"
Matthew 21:28–31

CHAPTER 8

Don't Use This Toolbox!

"If you do that again, I will throw you out the window," Charlene told Davy, her four-year-old son.

Davy was teasing the other children in the room, which distracted the moms gathered for Bible study. Davy looked at his mother, grinned, and ran off whooping like an Indian.

Charlene threw her hands in the air and looked at all of us, and said, "Now what am I supposed to do?"

Charlene, who was hosting the Bible study, was married to a man who served in the military, and they lived in housing on the base where he served. The unit they lived in had a big picture window in the living room. You could open each side of the window to get fresh air.

I (Carla) sat there looking at the window and started laughing. When asked what was so funny, I told Charlene if she said she was going to throw him out the window again (which we knew she would as we had heard her make this same threat many times before), she should pick him up and throw him out the window. It was less than a foot to the ground, covered with small bushes. All the moms looked at me like I was crazy, so I just shrugged and went on with the study.

It was not long before Davy came running through the house again, leading a charge of several other young boys, knocking over a lamp and disrupting our study again.

Charlene yelled, "David, if you do that again, I am going to throw you out... the... window."

She looked at me, realizing how many times she did say this, and shook her head as she went over to the window, took off the screen, picked up her son, and threw him into the bushes.

Davy was so stunned that he didn't make a sound. He stood up, turned around, and looked at his mom and said, "You threw me out the window!"

Charlene said, "Well, I told you I would." She sat down, picked up her Bible, and told us to go on to the next question.

Needless to say, she did not have another problem with Davy the rest of the morning. All the moms there learned a lesson that day which had nothing to do with the study.

Our son was two-and-a-half years old. The threat Michael heard from me the most was, "If you do that again, you will go to bed early, and I mean it this time."

I rarely followed through on this threat. Michael hated to go to bed. When I tried to put him to bed early he pitched such a fit it was exhausting dealing with his temper tantrum and it just wasn't worth it.

Have you heard the term, "idle threat?" The word "idle" means something is not moving. Idle threats are just words, nothing more because the person who gives them has no intention of following through with them.

When we gathered for the Bible study the next week, the big topic of discussion was how many threats we all used that our kids knew we weren't going to follow through on. We wondered why we kept giving threats to our kids, knowing the threats were not going to change their behavior.

What Good Are Threats?

Threats are negative in nature, as parents are usually yelling in frustration when they give them and their tone of voice is hard. If you get any results from threats, they are short term.

One of the chores we had given our son Michael when he was a teenager was to get the trash can out for collection each week. On Monday night, the trash can had to be taken out of the garage and pulled around to the alley to be picked up early the next morning. Michael rarely remembered to get this done. Even his sisters would remind him on Monday that it had to be taken out, but Michael would get busy with school, band and his other activities and forget to take it out.

I (Joey) yelled at him, threatened him, and yelled at him some more, to no avail. He just didn't get it done. He would lose the freedom of something he liked to do, which would make him get the trash out that week, but it had no lasting effect as he would forget to do it again the next week. This went on and on for months.

We would work with him to come up with a way to remind himself to get this chore done. He would put a note on his bedroom door, to no avail. The tension in my relationship with him over this chore was palpable and affected the entire family. We all dreaded Monday nights.

I would go out to the garage to see if he put out the trash can, come back in and the conflict would begin. Our girls would run and hide in their room. Something had to give.

God has a way of smacking me behind the head, and it happened this time as I made the offhand comment to my son about a different issue. I told him he had to say what he meant and mean what he said. As those words came out of my mouth, I felt like I had been hit by lightning. "Say what you mean, and mean what you say." I got it.

That next week, I didn't go out and check to see if the trash can was in the alley. Carla reminded me to go check, but I told her to let it go. I didn't remind Michael to do it. I did not say a word about the trash, which took every ounce of self-discipline I possessed.

When I saw the full trash can in the garage the next morning, I told Michael he was going to have to take the trash to the landfill that afternoon when school was over for the day.

Michael had the use of a car that we had owned for over a decade. He kept it spotless, and he was very proud of the car. He asked if he could use his mom's van to take the trash to the landfill. I told him he could not. So he loaded the stinky, dirty trash can into his car and took off for the landfill. He didn't miss putting out the trash again. Say what you mean, and mean what you say.

Blah, Blah, Blah

During those months of our tension-filled trash experience, when I (Joey) wasn't yelling at Michael or threatening him, I was lecturing him, another go-to from this toolbox you should get rid of.

"Michael, how many times have I told you to get the trash out? C'mon, you are a smart kid. What is it going to take to get this imprinted in your memory bank? You will be doing this chore the rest of your life if you don't start remembering to get it taken out. How are you going to hold down a job when you grow up if you can't remember what you are supposed to do?"

When you were lectured as a kid, did you listen to what your parents were telling you? If so, you are in the minority. If not, why do you think your kids are listening to you? Just like the other things we will mention in this chapter, it is just talk.

Your kids know what tools are in this toolbox too, and they know when you are going to do anything that will cause them pain. They also know from experience that you probably won't even remember what you told them once you get busy with your day. Lectures are a waste of time, words that go in one ear and out the other. Blah, blah, blah.

What Lectures Don't Do

Lectures don't give kids information they do not already have and most likely have already heard many times before. As parents, we think we will motivate our children to do the right thing with our great knowledge, experience, and oratory skills. When was the last time one of your children changed the direction he was going in because of a lecture you gave him?

So, what are you teaching your children when you lecture them? You are teaching them that their naughty or rebellious behavior will just get a slap on the wrist, but nothing more and certainly not enough pain to get them to change their behavior.

When you want to lecture your children, think of what you want to say and how to word it in *questions* that will lead them to confess their sin. I (Carla) was the lecture queen. When I got on a roll, I didn't stop. My kids just nodded their heads in agreement, told me they would work on it, and went on their merry way.

I remember the time I gave Briana a blistering lecture for something she didn't do completely. Not finishing this particular task the way it was supposed to be done was getting to be a habit with her. When I was done with my lecture, one of her siblings walked by and asked her what was going on. When I heard her say, "Mom's mad again about something I didn't do. She'll get over it." I knew then I needed to stop lecturing. I might feel smug after delivering one, but the recipient was obviously unaffected by them.

Writing down the points of the lecture helped me word it in questions to put in my memory bank for the upcoming conversation with the child who was in trouble. Joey showed me how to word the questions in such a way they got the offending child to back himself into a corner he could not get out of.

Questions, Questions

Of course, when you are asking questions that you want honest answers for, you must remain calm when you ask them and don't get defensive or angry when you hear responses you don't like.

The questions you ask your children seven years and up should be worded in such a way as to reveal whether your child understands the moral reasons behind what you have been training him in. If he doesn't, then you know he needs more teaching in that area.

What's a moral reason? It explains, from God's point of view, why we need to live our lives a certain way.

Simple questions work best for children under seven years of age so young children understand what you are asking them.

Friends of ours from another state were visiting for a couple days. I was watching the mom work with Joel, her seven-year-old son. He was in trouble again for being rude.

His mom would sit him at the kitchen table and quote 1 Corinthians 13:5, *"Love is not rude."*

She would tell him to sit until he had self-control and was ready to apologize for being rude. When he apologized and she asked him what rude thing he did, he told her he didn't know, and off he went to sit again.

Something was bothering me (Carla) each time this scenario played out. So I asked Joel if he knew what the word "rude" meant. He looked up and said he knew it was a bad word because his mom really didn't like it. I looked at his mom and said, "He's seven, why would he know what "rude" means?" Wise parents use terminology appropriate to their kids' ages or know when they need to define a word for them.

What's the Magic Word?

The military wives in the Bible study we shared about at the beginning of this chapter took their kids to the playground, and I (Carla) was glad to be invited to join them. The moms sat the kids at the picnic table to feed them the lunches we brought along. After the group prayer, you could hear moms saying, "What's the magic word?" before giving their children the food.

Does prompting children to say "please" when they want something work? It didn't work with two-and-a-half year old Michael. Instead, he would grab the food and stuff it in his mouth while I was trying to get it back until he said "please."

Remember the drill sergeant's conversation about boot camp? The military knows you can't train men on the battlefield. When you prompt your kids, you are urging them to do or say the right thing at the moment it needs to be done. By doing this you have created a battlefield your child will gladly meet you on, because when parents try to get their child to do or say the right thing when it needs to be done, this all too often leads to power struggles with the parents throwing in the towel long before their child will.

Prompting is an embarrassing tool for parents to use. Parents prompt their children when they are in a public situation because they want others to be impressed with their children's manners. When their children won't comply, red-faced parents become angrier than the situation calls for, and the resulting scene is not pleasant.

Prompting is another tool parents all too often fall back on that we encourage you to throw into the increasingly cluttered box of useless and ineffective tools.

Wouldn't it be better to ask your children before you get out of the car what the polite thing to do is when they are offered food? When you get the correct answer, ask your child if you can trust him to be polite when he gets around other people. Ask him what you should do if he isn't polite. You might be surprised by the answers you receive.

When Prompting Helps

Is there a time for prompting? When you are training your children to new behaviors and moral values, prompting becomes a helpful asset to have in your box of recommended tools.

We offer a different twist to prompting when you are training your children to a new behavior. Don't urge them to say or do the right thing in the moment it is required. We recommend you try this instead.

You are riding in the car with six-year-old Caden. The two of you have been talking about the day's events. Remembering Caden had difficulty coming when you called his name that morning, you ask him what he is supposed to do when you call his name. He gives you the right answer, so you talk about what he can do to work on remembering to do it when you call him.

By doing this, you are using a time of *no conflict* to prompt Caden to think about what he is to do when he hears his name called. Talking when no one is uptight, in a hurry, or has other things to do is an amazingly effective way to see fruit the next time your child's name is called.

Now that we have shown you threatening, lecturing, and prompting are not the best tools for successful parenting, you are most likely wondering what is next. This one is huge, and every parent is guilty of using this non-recommended tool of parenting all too often. Does that mean it works? You tell us.

Reminders... Reminders... Reminders

"Sam, have you done your homework yet?"

"Don't forget your report is due, Kayla. You need to get started on it."

"It's your turn to empty the dishwasher, Sophie."

"Wash your hands, William. It's time to eat."

Reminders, reminders, reminders. What's wrong with reminding your kids to get their stuff done? For one thing, reminders often turn into lectures, and we already know those don't work. Let's look at what is right about reminding your kids.

When Reminders Are a Good Tool

Assuming you have decided to use the guidelines presented in this book to train your children to obey, you and your spouse sit your children down to explain to them what you will require of them, using role-play to make sure they understood what this looks like.

You have been working on it for a few days now, and your four-year-old daughter Andrea comes when you call her but forgets to say "Yes, Mom" about half of the time. Your six-year-old son Ben yells "What?!" when you call his name one-third of the time. You and your spouse have been consistent with consequences. You wonder why they aren't getting it.

Your kids still need reminders and prompting. When you are training children of any age to a new behavior or moral value, they will need reminders and prompting until responding in this new way becomes a habit to them.

So how do we think you should remind your children when you are training them to a new behavior? Remind them by *asking questions*. What does this look like?

Five-year-old Caitlynn comes to you when you call her name with a smile on her face but doesn't remember to say, "Yes, Mommy, I'm coming."

When reminding the old way, you would say, "Caitlynn, you are supposed to say, 'Yes, Mommy, I'm coming' when I call your name. You need to remember to say it next time I call you."

When reminding the new way, you would gently take her chin in your hand and turn her face to look you in the eye. "Caitlynn, what are you supposed to say when I call your name?"

She tells you she is supposed to say, "Yes, Mommy, I'm coming."

You let her know you are going to try it again.

Caitlynn goes back to the other room, and when you call her name, she comes to you and says, "Yes, Mommy, I'm coming!" Words of praise and encouragement from you will go a long way to encourage her to come this way the next time you call her.

Older children will understand what you are instructing them to do faster than their younger siblings will. Older children may not show you they understand however, and parents quickly get discouraged.

Your children will test you to see if you mean business. How long and how hard they will test you depends on what you have done in the past. Your children will make your life miserable until you give up. If you have a history of giving up, you can count on this happening once you start training them to something new.

Don't Give Up!

What can you do about it? Don't give up! Who is in control? Who is the authority in the house? Be the rooster and take control of your chickens. Take away privileges and freedoms they have, and don't give them back until your kids give in.

Think of it this way. If you are not willing to give them painful consequences when they misbehave, then your only option left is to put up with their bad behavior.

Before you start working on a new behavior, you must decide you are going to be more stubborn than your children are and commit yourself to pray for perseverance, determined you will not give in again.

Reminding is also a good tool to use in your home when your children are overly tired or not feeling well. If your children are characterized by doing a chore well and forget for a day, this is another time that your child appreciates a reminder, or better yet, let it go and give them the gift of grace.

Bye, Bye Reminders

When your children over six years of age remember to come when you call their name half of the time, it is time for reminders and prompting to leave your home. A friend asked if I (Carla) could watch her young sons while she went to an out-of-town appointment. Five-year-old Caleb and three-year-old Micah came over for the day.

I was getting lunch on the table when Micah said, "I'm hungry! Can I have a sandwich?"

He was already pulling a sandwich I had just made off the serving plate. Because his mom asked me to reinforce what she was working on with him, I removed his hand from the plate and told him he could not have the sandwich.

Surprised, he immediately said, "Do you want me to say please?"

I asked him why he didn't say it when he knew he should have. He told me he always forgot to say it.

I said I didn't think it was important enough for him to remember since he didn't say "please" when he knew he should and told him to go sit in the other room and quietly look at books until I called him.

I waited about ten minutes and called his name. He came to me, sat at the table, and immediately asked for his food, remembering to say "please." I gladly gave him his lunch and praised him for choosing to say please.

So why do we remind our kids when it would be better if we didn't? For one thing, it is easy. We remind them and move on. It goes back to how busy our lives are. If a task is not done, Mom reminds her child to get it done. Taking on kids for not getting something done is usually messy and not fun for anyone involved, particularly the parent. Plus, taking on your kids takes time that very busy parents don't always have.

Because reminding will not get your kids to choose to remember what they need to be doing, it would be good if parents can get their schedules under control so they have time to work on these things with their kids.

Too Many Tools?

When you add the tools of counting to three, delayed obedience, misusing grace, allowing a bad attitude and partial obedience to the ones you have heard about in this chapter, we are sure you are thinking there are way too many things in this box of "Do not use" tools. There are, and that is why the tools in this box are so easy to fall back on when you are tired and frustrated and need to deal with your kids.

Planting Weeds

We told a story a couple chapters ago about an employee pulling weeds at the library. How do the weeds get there? Nobody wants to plant weeds in their yard, much less in their vegetable or flower garden.

Parents, however, are responsible for planting the majority of weeds in the hearts of their children. Ineffective methods of parenting are the culprits here. When you yell at your kids and threaten them in anger and frustration, you are planting very sturdy, hard-to-pull weeds in the garden of their hearts. They build walls to protect themselves from your angry and hurtful words. Think about it. Is your tongue a tool of righteousness or a weapon of destruction?

When you lecture your kids, you are planting weeds that multiply quickly with meaningless words. Instead, use your words to direct your children to one of God's principles of truth. Instead of saying, "Why do you have to hit your brother when he takes your toy?" try saying, "Name one kind thing you could do for your brother" (Ephesians 4:32). After you get a response, add, "Can you do this right now?"

When you prompt and remind your kids, you plant weeds down deep where they will reap a harvest that needs someone in authority following them around to pull them up.

Forget the rafters of the attic! Bury this toolbox in the backyard. Put a grave marker on it, and visit it once in a while as a reminder not to use the tools in it ever again. Keep going back to the toolbox in your home with the successful tools of parenting in it!

Excellent Words

Parents, your kids do listen to you. You are training them to parent your grandchildren one day. How you parent is likely how they will parent. They look to you for advice and guidance. When all they hear are lectures, threats, prompting, and reminders, they will start to look elsewhere for the leadership and wisdom they seek. The following is from the book, *Wisdom for Parents*.

> *"Hear, for I will speak of excellent things;*
> *and the opening of my lips shall be right things."*
> *Proverbs 8:6*

Are you worth listening to? Think of it. Your child looks to you for the answers to life. If you fail to speak excellent things, you do them a grave disservice. Here, Solomon encourages his children to listen because he speaks excellent and right things. Only excellent and right words are worth listening to. What is excellent speech? The word "excellent" in this passage is found forty-eight other times in the Old Testament, and in every other instance it refers to leaders or nobles. Thus, excellent speech is that which is noble and worthy of our submission. It is something worth listening to.[2]

Threatening, lecturing, and reminding are all part of the sin nature that comes naturally to us. Excellent speech does not. It takes work and requires time spent in the Word of God. Please remember that parenting your children is a season of your life. The time will come all too quickly when they will be gone from your home.

Once they are gone, there will be time to invest in your favorite activities, hobbies, and such. The time you take to spend with your children now and effectively train them in the character of Christ will reap eternal rewards.

Kids Can't Get Enough of Praise and Encouragement

When Briana was around twelve years old, she had lost most of her freedoms for an overall lack of responsibility. One day when she was getting another lecture from me (Carla), she asked if I ever noticed when she did anything good.

I started crying as I pulled her into my arms to give her a hug. I went up to my room and started making a list of the things my kids did well. We were working on the big things our children were misbehaving in, so I looked for the little things they were doing right.

Briana made her bed and had her quiet time every morning without fail. Amy was the encourager in the family. Had we ever thanked her for this? Michael was dependable and protective of his sisters.

Using notecards, I wrote one good thing they did in the form of praise or encouragement in each card. The next morning, they each found one on their placemat at breakfast.

Leaving one for them where they could find it whenever they were in trouble gave us the assurance they would always know we saw the good in them and we loved them.

Our marriage benefitted when Joey started finding notes letting him know ways he was appreciated. My heart was full of joy when our kids started writing cards or notes and leaving them for us when we were having a bad day. Briana taught us a hard lesson that day, and we have never forgotten it.

We have talked a lot about how to get your kids to obey and how to give them pain when they don't comply. Please don't forget children need praise and encouragement to survive.

The Helpful Toolbox

So what are the tools we have talked about that belong in the toolbox you want to use when you parent?

- Routine

- Consequences: Taking away what your child misused, sitting, natural consequences and spanking

- Tough Love

- Parent on the same page

- Praise and encouragement

- Excellent words

Our family was in a destructive cycle. When our ten-year-old daughter would show disrespect or disobedience, we would let it go until we got fed up and things would explode. We would yell at each other, and there would be long lectures into late hours of the night with angry eyes from our preteen. Our relationship with our daughter was growing more distant, and our marriage was suffering from us not being on the same page on how to parent her. We were desperate.

This is when we turned to Joey and Carla for counseling. We did everything they suggested wholeheartedly, and little by little, day by day, we started to see results from our consistent and persistent parenting. There were major battles at first, but as we stood our ground and our daughter saw we were serious, we finally saw consistent obedience from her. We were finally able to cultivate a relationship of trust with her. We discovered rules without relationships equal rebellion. She became teachable, and we were able to train her heart.

She is now sixteen years old, and the random hugs and "I love you, Mom and Dad" throughout the day are priceless to us. She has thanked us for taking the time to teach her these principles. I cringe to think of the devastation that would have crippled our family if we didn't have the courage to fight for the obedience of our daughter. It was well worth it, and I thank God for allowing us to have a beautiful and fun relationship with her now.

—Paul and Jodi, Iowa

"Whoever loves discipline loves knowledge,
but he who hates correction is stupid."
Proverbs 12:1

CHAPTER 9

It's Not Too Late

Doug and Brenda were having many issues with their fifteen-year-old son. He wasn't responding to them or doing what they asked of him. They felt like he was running their home, and life wasn't enjoyable with him in the house. They became convinced they did not have a standard of obedience with him, and they wanted to do something about it.

They began working on this with urgency because they knew re-training a teenager was not going to be easy. It was a difficult task, but they stuck with it. They did make progress, and their son finally started submitting to them.

A few years later, Doug and his son started a business together in a field they were both very skilled at. This young man is now married and a father of three children. His parents have wondered what their relationship with their son would be like if they had never realized what obedience truly was and had not diligently worked on getting it with him. Both Doug and Brenda agree that Doug and their son would have never been able to work together if their son had not learned to obey and respect them, nor did Doug think he would have a relationship with his son today.

It is our hope and prayer that you are now thinking, "I can get my kids to behave!" However, what we all too often hear is, "My child is too old. It's too late for us." Really? When we ask how old the child in question is, often the answer is somewhere between seven and twelve years of age.

Your children have most of their lives ahead of them. If it is too late, who will teach your children to pay attention to speed limits when they start driving? How is it possible they can hope to remain pure until they marry, for we all know how much self-control it takes?

Why would they think they have to listen to anyone in authority, including future employers? If it will give them an edge, why shouldn't they cheat on their tests?

You think we are being overly dramatic? When will they magically decide they need to obey laws and people in authority? We have counseled many Christian parents who struggled with issues just like these. If asked, they would readily tell you they wish they had taught their children differently when they were young.

If your children won't obey you, then they don't respect you. If they won't obey you and don't respect you, they are not going to listen to you when you try to teach them the moral values of life you want and expect them to live by.

Who will teach them to be kind? Our son, being almost five years older than his closest sister in age, didn't have a lot of patience for his sisters at times and frequently showed it. We told him they were God's practice field for marriage. If he couldn't treat them kindly when they were irritating him, would he treat his future wife with respect when she irritated him? We used the phrase, "Good, better, and best" in our parenting.[1]

Good, Better and Best

"Good" represents the minimum you can give considering the context of the moment. The minimum we tolerated from Michael was something that was kind in action. "Better" represented just that, something better than the minimum. In this situation, "better" would include kindness in both action and words. "Best" was near the maximum of what you could do in a given moment.

At times, Michael would walk by us and mutter, "Good is all the girls will get today." On those days it was good enough, as we watch how he treasures and nurtures his wife today.

Who will teach your kids not to hold grudges when someone offends them? Briana, our middle daughter, had problems with this. She would not speak to the offender, or she was rude when she was mad at him/her. We worked with her over the course of her high school years to resolve differences rather than hold a grudge.

She thought she had the right to stay mad until the offender apologized to her, and if she didn't like his apology, she would stay angry until she decided to forgive him. I (Carla) told her she was elevating herself to a peer level with God. If He unconditionally forgives us for any sin we have committed when we ask Him to, then what right does she have to withhold forgiveness when it was asked of her?

I also shared with her few adults apologize, partly because adults are rarely aware when they offend someone. She could marry someone whose parents had not taught the value of an apology. What would she do then? It took time, but we did see progress.

So, who will teach and train your children if you don't? No matter the age of your child, it is not too late for you to take this responsibility on. Will it be more difficult the older they are? Yes, but it is not impossible.

One Thing at a Time

Once again, we want to encourage you to focus and work on one thing at a time. We cannot stress this enough. This is the only way to be successful when you are starting to train your kids to obey you.

When Robb and Jan married, they were excited about life. Robb had just finished Bible College, and they were looking forward to a wonderful life and ministry together. They couldn't wait to start their family.

When Jan was expecting their first child, they read many parenting books and took parenting classes. They were as ready as any two people could be to welcome this little one into their family. What they weren't ready for was how to apply what they had learned.

They called one day when their daughter was nine years old. Robb and Jan were frustrated because their daughter would not do what they told her to do and she was not quiet about it. After working with them for six months, they shared this with us.

One thing that really helped us was knowing we had the freedom to work on one thing at a time. How I wish we would have realized this earlier in our parenting. We thought we had to be correcting for everything our kids did wrong or we were letting them get away with something. Working on one thing at a time has really helped all of us to be less frustrated, and we are finally seeing progress with our daughter.

Me, Obey?

You cannot ask your kids to do what you yourself are not doing. You tell your child to tell the person at the door that you are not home. Your five-year-old does not understand the man at the door wants to sell you something you don't want. She thinks you just asked her to lie for you when you had dealt with her firmly for lying the day before.

Your seven-year-old hit his younger sister. You grab him by his arms and, through gritted teeth demand to know why he can't be kind to his sister. He lets you know he will be kind to his sister when you are kind to him.

Your sixteen-year-old is an hour late getting home. You give her a verbal thrashing for being late when she reminds you that you didn't call when you were two hours late getting home the other day. She tells her friends her parents are hypocrites, fakes, and phonies.

Are you getting the picture? It smarts, doesn't it? So, how well does obedience and submission characterize you? We learned a long time ago that our children learn more from what we do than what we say. Do your actions speak louder than words?

Take a few minutes right now and think of areas in your life that could use improvement according to how the Bible tells us to live. Pick one, and come up with a plan to get to work on it right away.

If you have older children or teens, you might need to apologize to them for the lack of obedience in your own life. This could be the trigger for them to begin working on things in their life.

Dad to Dad (From Joey to Dads)

Often, it is moms who read books on marriage and parenting. I (Joey) know dads can be irritated when their wives try to share new things they want to try from reading a book like this. However, just the fact your wife is willing to read something on parenting means she is probably not happy with the way things are going in your home. That should concern you.

Do your children play you against each other, knowing you will get your wife to back down on giving a consequence? Do your children know exactly what buttons to push to get you to throw your hands in the air and walk away?

If this describes your home, please take a few minutes and read Chapter 5 in this book if you haven't already. If you don't get a biblical standard of obedience from your children, it will not be long before they will stop listening to anything you have to say, and you will become frustrated and will likely react in a way you won't be proud of.

Men, are your wives frustrated with your child's level of obedience? Do your children show respect to her? Let me ask you honestly, Dad. If you were in the store or walking at a sports event, would you let people speak to your wife the way your children do? I am often surprised and disappointed at the way some fathers let their children speak to their mothers.

In Ephesians 6:1, we are told that children need to obey their parents. In the next verse, they are told to honor their father and their mother. *"Honor your father and mother—which is the first commandment with a promise—that it may go well with you and that you may enjoy long life on the earth"* (Ephesians 6:2). To show "honor" to a person is to present to them *"excellence of character; to esteem them highly."*[2]

It is your job Dad to be sure your children are speaking to their mother with a good attitude that shows respect and are obeying her just as you expect them to obey you. If they don't, by dishonoring her, they are also dishonoring you.

If your children look down on your wife, I respectfully ask you to consider this to be your wake-up call to deal with it. With the bases loaded, it is time to step up to the plate, Dad, and tackle these issues with your children head-on so they will demonstrate love to and for your wife, who is their mother.

While you will get a lot of mileage out of this with your wife, you will also be showing your sons how to treat their wives someday and your daughters how they should expect their husbands to treat them. Always try to keep the big picture in mind.

If your child will not back down from arguing with your wife when she is asking him to, then, as head of the home, step in. Make sure you and your wife agree first that this is acceptable to her.

When dads step in, some women see this as an indication they are weak. This is not how children see it, especially your firstborn. They see their dad telling them (their kids) they are wrong, and it does make a difference to your kids.

You are the protector of the home, and when you step in, you are protecting your wife, letting your children know you will not let them dishonor or disrespect her by not obeying her in action and attitude.

On another note, do not get into arguments with your children. If you find yourself yelling at them and arguing with them, I know it is because you are frustrated with their behavior and tired from your day at work and all you want to do is relax.

Unfortunately, the damage we do to the hearts and souls of our children by showing them how angry we are is often insurmountable. You need to eliminate criticism, harping on a child's weaknesses and derogatory remarks from your parenting.

Walk away, and ask your wife to step in and take over with the child. Find a way to calm yourself down. When you are calm, tackle the issue again, looking for the root cause rather than continuing to deal with surface issues the root grows to become. I can't tell you enough how I wish I had paid more heed to this when I was raising my children.

If you have not seen the movie *Courageous*, please consider renting it soon. If it has been a while since you saw it, I would recommend you get it and watch it again. This quote comes from the talk the central character gave at his church on Father's Day.

> *I don't want to be a good enough father. We have a few short years to influence our kids. Whatever patterns we set for them in life will be used for their kids, and the generation after that. We have the responsibility to mold a life, and I don't think that should be done casually. Half the fathers in this country are already failing, and I don't want to be one of them. I'm talking about setting the standards your kids need to aim for in life.*[3]

I wrote this thought down the last time I saw this movie. "There will come a point when a man realizes his job and his hobbies have no eternal value, but the hearts and the souls of his children do."

By God's Design

Why should parents put in all this work to raise an obedient child? Answering this question may help provide you with endurance and perseverance through the difficult times you will have in training your child to be obedient.

We believe every child is created by God's design. Just as God visited Mary and Joseph to give them His own Son whom they would raise, we believe God gave His blessing to the children He has given you. The way your child is, in his character, physical perfections, as well as imperfections, they were all created just as God designed for your child and His glory.[3]

In Judges 13, we learn about a man named Samson. Like John the Baptist, Samson's parents had been unable to bear a child, and they were getting old. An angel of the Lord appeared to Samson's mother-to-be and told her she was going to bear a child and it would be a boy. The angel told her to drink no wine during her pregnancy, and she was never to cut his hair, for her son would become a Nazirite.

God would not have asked Samson's parents to do this if He did not already know they would obey. For Samson, this was a lifelong vow of no alcohol and no haircuts. God pledged this vow in Samson's name before he was born. God wanted to use him to rescue the Israelites from the Philistines, where they had been perishing for forty years.

Now, why are we telling you the story of Samson? We firmly believe that, just as God had Samson's (and John the Baptist's) life mapped out before they were conceived, He also has a plan and purpose for your children's lives. Part of that plan was putting them in your family so you can train them the way God wants them to be so they will be ready to do what He created them for.

He chose you to raise your children because He knew you can and will raise them to shine His light to a world bent on doing things their own way. Do you realize you are God's tool to sharpen and train your children? It is up to you to choose to be a tool worthy of His respect.

What does God want to do with the children He has blessed you with? If your children do not know how to be obedient, it is not likely they will listen to what God's plan for them is. Samson but he had a weakness for women, and one of them destroyed him. This was the sad result of Samson's partial obedience.

We think this is a pretty big reason why all parents, especially Christian ones, need to teach their children how to obey, for they will do the right thing when they obey.

Your children will learn to obey you, and through a relationship of trust with you their parents, they will understand their need to obey God. With three adult children who are following the Lord in their lives, we affirm what John wrote in his third letter, a testimony every parent would like to share one day.

"I have no greater joy than to hear that
my children are walking in the truth"
3 John 1:4

Imagine the joy in Hannah's heart as she watched God use her son Samuel to lead Israel out of one of the most turbulent times in its history. During that time, Samuel anointed Saul and later David to be the kings of Israel.

May you share this same joy as you train your children to be obedient and help them grow and mature into adults whose lives reflect the glory of Christ because you trained them to follow young Samuel's example of obedience.[5]

I was born in Iran and brought up as a Muslim. When I was about fifteen years old, I came to America to be educated and met a wonderful American woman. We married and had two children who we brought up the best we knew how. In my mid-thirties, I came to know Christ as my personal savior, and God blessed us with two more children. With the teaching shared in this book, we learned to bring them up to a biblical standard of obedience we had not known to do before. We now have the privilege of bringing up our eleven-year-old grandson, and this teaching is proving to be invaluable to us once again. We thank God for the Links and their willingness to put their hearts and souls into working with families.

—Tony and Terri, Illinois

"For wisdom will come into your heart,
and knowledge will be pleasant to your soul;
discretion will watch over you, understanding will
guard you, delivering you from the way of evil."
Proverbs 2:10-12

NOTES

Chapter 1

1. Daniel Webster, *Webster's New Collegiate Dictionary* (Springfield, MA: G. & C. Merriam Co., 1951), 60.

2. Ibid., 579.

3. John Gill, *Gill's Exposition of the Entire Bible* (London: Matthew & Leigh,1810), 76.

Chapter 2

1. Gary and Anne Marie Ezzo, *Growing Kids God's Way* (Louisiana, MO: Growing Families Int'l, 1988, 1992, 1997, 2002, 2007), 123–129.

2. Joey and Carla Link, "Understanding Freedoms, Part 1 and Part 2," in *Mom's Notes Volume 1* (Burlington, IA: J & C Ministries Mom's Notes, 1996, 2002).

3. Joey and Carla Link, *Understanding First-Time Obedience Pack* (Burlington, IA: J & C Ministries Mom's Notes, 1999, 2008). This kit comes with CDs, notes, and a laminated chart that is a quick reference for parents when training their kids to obedience.

Chapter 3

1. Carla Link, "Structure and Routine," in *The Toddlerhood Transitions, Parenting Your Eighteen to Thirty-Six Month*

Old (Louisiana, MO: Growing Families Int'l, 2009), 57–63.

2. Joey and Carla Link, "Structuring Your Children's Day, Part 1 and Part 2," in *Mom's Notes Volume 1* (Burlington, IA: J & C Ministries Mom's Notes, 1998, 2001).

3. Daniel Webster, 236.

4. Iowa Department of Human Services, *Foster Parent Handbook*, 179.

5. Proverbs 13:24, Proverbs 22:15, Proverbs 23: 13–14, Proverbs 29:15, I Corinthians 2:21, Hebrews 12:6, Hebrews 12:11

6. Carla Siemens Link, Bachelor of Science degree in social work (Chico, CA: California State University, 1977).

7. Proverbs 6:16–19

8. Iowa Department of Human Services, "Standards for Foster Parents under Iowa Law," in *Foster Parent Handbook*, 179.

Chapter 4

1. Daniel Webster, 358.

2. 1 Samuel 15:10–11

Chapter 5

1. Joey and Carla Link, "Parenting as Partners," in *Mom's Notes Volume 4* (Burlington, IA: J & C Ministries Mom's Notes, 2002).

2. Lysa TerKeurst, *Am I Messing Up My Kids?* (Eugene, OR: Harvest House Publishers, 2012).

3. Tim LaHaye, *Spirit-Controlled Temperaments* (Wheaton, IL: Tyndale House Publishers, 1966, 2002, 2004), 1–2.

4. Joey and Carla Link, "Ten Ways to Fight Fair with Your Spouse," in *Mom's Notes Volume 3* (Burlington, IA: J & C Ministries Mom's Notes, 1999).

Chapter 6

1. Joey and Carla Link, "Using the Bible in the Instruction and Training of Your Children," in *Mom's Notes Volume 4* (Burlington, IA: J & C Ministries Mom's Notes,1995).

2. Sleep Disorders Center of Virginia, "Sleep Facts," www.sleepcenter.org.

3. Joey and Carla Link, "Discipline Issues" in *Mom's Notes Volume 3* (Burlington, IA: J & C Ministries Mom's Notes, 1999).

4. Frank Hamrick, *Wisdom for Parents* (Whitakers, NC: Positive Action for Christ, 2008), 22.

Chapter 7

1. Joey and Carla Link, "Working with Your Child's Besetting Sins, Parts 1,2,3," in *Mom's Notes Volume 2* (Burlington, IA: J & C Ministries Mom's Notes, 1998). These presentations (on CD) help parents better understand the weaknesses of their children's temperaments and how to work with them.

2. Gary Smalley and John Trent, *The Treasure Tree* (Nashville, TN: W Publishing Group, 1992).

3. Daniel Webster, 615.

4. Joey and Carla Link, "Training the Passive Rebellious Child," in *Mom's Notes Volume 4* (Burlington, IA: J & C Ministries Mom's Notes, 2002).

Chapter 8

1. King James Version, Cambridge Edition, online text by Bibleprotectors.com.

2. Frank Hamrick, *Wisdom for Parents* (Whitakers, NC: Positive Action for Christ, 2008), 41.

Chapter 9

1. Gary and Anne Marie Ezzo, 220.

2. Daniel Webster, 397.

3. *Courageous*, 2011.

4. John 9:1

5. 1 Samuel 3

Additional Resources by Joey and Carla Link

Study questions for each chapter of this book can be downloaded at www.parentingmadepractical.com. Check this website often for posts on parenting topics by Joey and Carla Link.

The *Mom's Notes* Parenting Presentations

Over forty *Mom's Notes* presentations on CD and in written form can be purchased individually, in sets, starter packs, or volumes at www.parentingmadepractical.com.

Available on CD and in written form, the *Mom's Notes* are practical parenting presentations on a variety of topics. The sessions are presented in age ranges from toddlers through the teen years so the application is age-appropriate. Although both Joey and Carla wrote all the presentations, they are called Mom's *Notes* because, for the most part, Carla presented them to Mom's Groups across the country. By no means are these presentations intended for moms only.

Topics include:

- Finding the Balance in Biblical Parenting, 3-Part Series

- Fundamentals

- Understanding First-time Obedience

- Discipline Issues

- It's All About Attitude

- Training Toddlers

- Training Preschoolers

- Training Elementary School Age Children

- Training Middle School Age Children

- Building a Relationship of Trust with a Rebellious Teen

- Understanding Character Training, Part 1 and Part 2

- Dealing with Sibling Conflict, Part 1 and Part 2

PARENTING RESOURCES
Recommended By Joey And Carla Link

- *To find Out about Growing Kids God's Way Parenting Classes,* www.GFI.org

- Gary Ezzo and Dr. Robert Bucknam, *On Becoming... Baby Wise, Toddlerwise, PreschoolWise, Childwise, Preteenwise,* and *TeenWise*

- Jill Savage— *No More Perfect Moms, Real Real Moms... Real Jesus, Professionalizing Motherhood*

- Pam Forster—*For Instruction in Righteousness*

- Kara Durbin,—*Parenting with Scripture*

- Kendra Smiley—*Be the Parent, Journey of the Strong-Willed Child*

- Chip Ingram—*Effective Parenting in a Defective World*

- George Barna—*Revolutionary Parenting*

- Frank Hamrick—*Wisdom for Parents*

- Sarah Mally— *Making Brothers and Sisters Best Friends*

- Jill Rigby—*Raising Respectful Children in a Disrespectful World, Raising Unselfish Children in a Self-Absorbed World*

Books for Teens, College Students, and Young Adults

Eric and Leslie Ludy— *When God Writes Your Love Story, The First 90 Days of Marriage*

Leslie Ludy— *Set-Apart Femininity, Authentic Beauty*

Eric Ludy—*God's Gift to Women*

Books on Temperaments

Tim LaHaye—*Spirit-Controlled Temperaments*

Gary Smalley and John Trent—*The Treasure Tree*

You will find these and many more resources at www. parentingmadepractical.com

About the Authors

Joey and Carla Link are parent educators who make parenting practical. Joey served for sixteen years as a youth and family pastor and has served for twenty years as the Director of Family Life Resources, a nonprofit ministry to families. Carla's degree is in social work. The Links have worked in association with Growing Families Int'l, an international parenting ministry for over two decades.

They have traveled extensively across the country teaching and speaking at churches, parenting conferences, and seminars. Together, they bring a unique and fresh blend of teaching to today's parents.

The Links live in Burlington, IA and have three grown children and one grandchild.

Contact Joey and Carla about speaking at your church, Parenting conference or seminar at www.parentingmadepractical.com